The New Inquisition

.

Praise for *The New Inquisition*

James LaRue's The New Inquisition: Understanding and Managing Intellectual Freedom Challenges *is a timely and valuable addition to the literature on combating the censorious tendency. It is timely because, though the censors, banners, and burners are always with us, we face particularly difficult challenges in the age of "the war on terror" and the rise of conservative religious forces in society. The classic reasons for censorship—obscenity, sedition, and blasphemy—have all raised their vile heads in this decade as prudes, authoritarians, and religious fundamentalists seek to limit the reading and viewing of others. It is part of the library faith that humans everywhere are entitled to freedom of thought and expression and those freedoms are curtailed if censors close lines of individual inquiry. That fundamental value is relatively easy to grasp but often difficult to implement in the face of real world pressures. LaRue shows us how to fight those real world fights effectively in a text written with panache and pungency. I recommend his book without reservation.*

> **—Michael Gorman**, Dean of Library Services, California State University, Fresno, and Immediate Past President, American Library Association

LaRue's "on the ground" perspective is imbued with a deep understanding of the historical and sociological context of censorship. He is at once passionate about the enduring ethics of human rights, and dispassionate about the process by which librarians must seek to protect these rights.

I anticipate assigning The New Inquisition *to graduate students studying to become librarians. It will give them tools to fight for First Amendment freedoms and the grace to deepen community understanding while they are at it.*

> **—Kathleen de la Peña McCook**, Distinguished University Professor, School of Library and Information Science, University of South Florida, Tampa

The New Inquisition

Understanding and Managing Intellectual Freedom Challenges

James LaRue

A Member of the Greenwood Publishing Group

Westport, Connecticut • London

Library of Congress Cataloging-in-Publication Data

LaRue, James, 1954-
   The new inquisition : understanding and managing intellectual freedom challenges /
James LaRue.
      p. cm.
   Includes bibliographical references and index.
   ISBN-13: 978-1-59158-285-4 (alk. paper)
   ISBN-10: 1-59158-285-7 (alk. paper)
   1. Public libraries—United States—Administration. 2. Libraries and community—
United States. 3. Intellectual freedom—United States. 4. Public libraries—Censorship—
United States. 5. Academic freedom—United States. I. Title.
   Z716.4.L37 2007
   025.1′974—dc22   2006102885

British Library Cataloguing in Publication Data is available.

Library of Congress Catalog Card Number: 2006102885
ISBN: 978-1-59158-285-4

First published in 2007

Libraries Unlimited, 88 Post Road West, Westport, CT 06881
A Member of the Greenwood Publishing Group, Inc.
www.lu.com

Printed in the United States of America

The paper used in this book complies with the
Permanent Paper Standard issued by the National
Information Standards Organization (Z39.48–1984).

10   9   8   7   6   5   4   3   2   1

To
William Henry Waack
Freethinker, Autodidact, Granddad

Contents

Acknowledgments

No book is the work of one person. I would like to acknowledge the insight—and patience!—of my editor, Barbara Ittner, without whom this book would never have come into focus.

I would like to thank the citizens of Douglas County, particularly those whose challenges to library materials and services gave me the opportunity to think deeply about the purpose of the public library in our society. I am also grateful to my Board, which has stood by me even when my own exercise of free speech made them distinctly uncomfortable. I have benefited from their wise advice.

I am indebted to the director and circulation staff of the University of Denver, who gave me free rein to their collection at just the moment when I needed it.

I would like to acknowledge the encouragement of my good friends David and Meg Truhler, who helped me through the day when I nearly gave up on this manuscript.

Many thanks, too, to Michal Rudolf, author of the Linux open source project KnowIt, currently the premier outliner in the Linux world. As I was revising the book, Michal was revising the program I was using to create it.

Finally, I would like to acknowledge the unfailing support of Suzanne, my best friend and my wife, whose warm presence, literate conversation, and occasional outrage at the world continue to charm and stimulate. She is a tonic for our times.

Introduction: The Blue Line

I was raised in Waukegan, Illinois, north of Chicago, along the shore of Lake Michigan. One day when I was about six, I was reluctantly playing in a neighborhood baseball game. On that muggy August day, I was stuck way out in right field. I mean way out—possibly Indiana. They didn't even bother to call me in to bat when my team was up; by the time I could walk in, it would be time to walk out again. I was hot and bored.

But I did have a view of Lewis Avenue and the line of stores there: a grocery store, a Walgreens, and a Woolworths.

Then I saw it. The heat was shimmering on the horizon, rising off the asphalt. It resolved into something big and blue, as large as a bus. Fascinated, I watched it pull into the grocery store parking lot.

It was a bookmobile.

I walked off the field (I wasn't missed) and went home. I got my mother to walk me over to the stores.

From the moment I stepped up into the bookmobile, I was in awe. A bus full of books! In a kind of stunned glee, I asked for and got a library card. They let me check out three books right on the spot. It was free!

Thus the bookmobile became a part of my life. It was there in the parking lot every week. And so was I.

On the second trip, I noticed a bright blue line painted around the whole inside of the bus, at about the top of the second set of shelves. I asked the librarian, Mrs. Johnson, what it meant.

She told me that everything below the blue line was for kids. Everything above the line was for adults. My first thought was, "How clever and how right! Adults are taller, so they get the high shelves."

For many weeks, I was content. There were so many beautiful books literally right on my level.

But gradually, I began to notice the differences between the children's books and the adult books. Adult books were thicker. They didn't have as many pictures. They had intriguing titles. For some reason, I still recall the buckram binding of *All Quiet on the Western Front* by Erich Remarque.

One day I picked up an adult book and tried to check it out. Mrs. Johnson wouldn't let me. By that time, my mother no longer came with me to the bookmobile. Without an adult's permission, I could only check out kids' books.

Frankly, I was outraged. If those books were forbidden to me, then clearly, those were the books I most needed to read.

There began months of guerrilla patronage. I began with simple attempts—choosing the fattest, dullest children's books I could find, and slipping the skinniest, most brightly covered adult book in between them. I'd wait until the line was long and it was almost time for the bookmobile to leave.

It never worked. Quietly and with a little smile, Mrs. Johnson would just set the book aside. Now, of course, I know she was looking for the letter "J" (for juvenile) on the book pocket. Back then, I thought it was either her highly detailed knowledge of each book on the bus or some kind of malicious psychic ability.

"Mrs. Johnson," I would say earnestly, "that's a kids' book!"

"No," she would say, with infuriating mildness. "It was above the blue line."

I became a librarian to find out what was over the line.

Eventually, I moved to a different neighborhood. The bookmobile didn't come there. But by then, I was hooked. So I walked or biked to the downtown library. I suspect that the rules changed about then; I don't recall being stopped from reading the many adult science fiction books I discovered there.

Eventually, Mrs. Johnson showed up downtown, too. I grew very fond of her. She gave me Plato and steered me to the new young adult section. I eventually went back to her for career advice and found her both sympathetic and wise.

But the memory of her earlier refusal to let me read what I wanted to had burned into my soul. I became convinced that there were hidden treasures in the library, books that told the searing truth. I would find them, no matter how many librarians sought to conceal them.

I was right, of course. There are indeed books of sweeping power and uncompromising clarity. These are the great books, the books that endure through the ages. These are the books written by Shakespeare, Mencken, Sinclair Lewis, Thoreau, Thomas Paine, and on and on.

These are also the books (and other services) that our citizens challenge time and again. There are things that anger and frighten and confuse.

And librarians do hide them, amid all the claptrap and happy talk and political correctness and diet books. Welcome to America.

The Need for and Purpose of This Book

As the following pages will show, censorship has always existed. But at the end of the twentieth century and the dawn of the twenty-first, there has been a surge of patron-initiated challenges to public library materials and services. These challenges have two distinct causes.

The first is a generational dynamic, manifesting itself in the following:

- A liberal or "politically correct" movement
- A conservative or "family-friendly" movement
- A parental profile among the nation's largest demographic of protectiveness, or even overprotectiveness

Together, these manifestations have resulted in a revaluing of many public institutions, including the public library.

The second is the birth of a new technology, the World Wide Web. The Web has greatly expanded access to human experience—even for the very young. One could argue, and I will, that that's precisely what technology does. The World Wide Web is but the latest example.

The reason for this book is that I passionately believe the library is worth preserving and advancing. The revaluing of the library is not, in itself, a bad thing. Institutions exist for people, not for the institutions themselves. But a failure to defend the library, an unwillingness to take the side of one of our most enduring, radical, and even essential public structures, would be a very bad thing.

To advance the value of the public library, its advocates must understand the deep meaning and purpose of the institution. They must understand the role of the library in today's society.

They must also familiarize themselves with core documents that articulate library principles. They must commit to adopting the best practices of policy and procedures.

It is also important to understand and actively experiment with new technologies. Finally, library advocates must truly engage with the local community, and even be willing to move to the legislative level and beyond.

Scope and Audience

This book is meant to provide enough historical context to set the stage for the topic and enough philosophy not to lose its way. But the essential offering is practical advice—primarily for public library administrators, governing boards, and line staff—on how to respond to public challenges.

CHAPTER 1

Background: A Historical Perspective

History of Censorship: The Burning of Books

Even before Gutenberg, there was censorship. Here are just a few instances of an extreme example: the burning of books. (Much of the following comes from Williams and Kamien 2002 and American Library Association 2002.)

- **213 BCE:** Sheh Huang-ti (also spelled Shi Huangdi) was responsible for one of the earliest recorded book burnings. He ordered the destruction by fire of all copies of the first anthology of Chinese poetry compiled by Confucius two hundred years earlier. Why? The Confucian scholars didn't like Sheh's dismantling of feudalism. Sheh Huang-ti struck back (Williams and Kamien 1999).

- **Third century CE?:** Alexandria's fabled library of some 700,000 scrolls was set aflame. Nobody is altogether sure who was responsible. Some say it was Julius Caesar, when he set fire to the city's harbor in 48 BCE, and it spread. Others say the Christians did it when converting the Temple of Serapis to a church. Finally, some lay the blame at the feet of the Muslim Caliph Omar. In 640 CE, the Muslims took the city of Alexandria. The Caliph is alleged to have said of the library's holdings, "They will either contradict the Koran, in which case they are heresy, or they will agree with it, so they are superfluous." So this library, widely regarded as the largest of antiquity, was destroyed by Romans (as collateral damage) or by Christians or Muslims for religious reasons. The crime was great, and the memory of it endures even though the criminals and their precise motives are unknown.

- **1139 CE:** Pope Innocent II torched the heretical writings of the eleventh-century French philosopher and theologian Abelard.

- **1240 CE:** King Louis IX (later known as Saint Louis for his zeal during the seventh and eighth Crusades) directed Dominican monks to burn the Talmud

(Jewish holy texts). Two popes upheld the tradition: Pope Gregory and Pope Julius called for the burning of the Talmud everywhere, the latter as recently as the 1500s.

Once the printing press caught on and the literate population surged, the task of censorship became both more urgent and more difficult.

It became more urgent because the more readily available information presented a profound threat to the prevailing power structure. According to Douglas McMurtrie in his history of printing, *The Book*, "Almost half of the books printed in the fifteenth century were religious in subject matter. . . . In the different dialects of German were issued fifteen editions of the Bible; in Italian, thirteen; in French, eleven; in Bohemian, two; and one each in Spanish and in Dutch."

All of a sudden, people didn't have to ask a priest what the Bible said about something or what it meant. They could read it and decide for themselves. One consequence of the printing press was the Protestant Reformation.

As censorship became more urgent, it also became more difficult because instead of just one collection of tomes in a single location, books were strewn like dandelion seeds in the wind, settling and sprouting anywhere, a wild and unruly profusion of print.

This combination of circumstances sparked paranoia in the Church elite, an escalation of fear, suspicion, and finally, official overreaction. As Monty Python put it, "No one expects the Spanish Inquisition." But that's what we got.

In the modern age, the theme of anti-Semitism continues. The most vivid example of book burning is that done by the Nazis.

But the practice did not end with the Nazis, nor has its only target been the books of Judaism. In 1993, John Birmingham, a Kansas City clergyman, burned two books donated by the gay community to high school libraries. Birmingham hoped to turn the tide against the growing acceptance of the gay community. He wasn't particularly successful, but he made headlines again in 1995 when he burned the Kansas City Public Library's copy of *The New Joy of Gay Sex* on the library steps.

More recently have been the jubilant bonfires of Harry Potter books because of their alleged celebration of witchcraft and the more curious "book cutting" of the so-called Jesus Party when the local fire department denied the group a fire permit in November 2001.

In short, books are sometimes literally a hot topic, as much so today as they were millennia ago. I'm tempted to argue that this is compelling evidence against evolution. On the other hand, as no less a person than Sigmund Freud put it in 1933, "What progress we are making. In the Middle Ages they would have burned me. Now they are content with burning my books."

He was wrong, of course.

Definitions

What Is Censorship?

Burning books, as in the cases above, is indeed censorship, but that is not the only form of censorship. What do we mean by censorship?

Censorship is the action by government officials to prohibit or suppress publications or services on the basis of their content.

These publications may be print, music, images, or electronic. The services may be Internet access or meeting rooms or art galleries. The distinguishing element of censorship is not format, but government action.

A private business may forbid its employees from wearing T-shirts or buttons with various messages, at least while those employees are at work. Private citizens may purchase, then destroy, copies of books they disapprove of. They may privately or publicly call for individual boycotts of books. Library patrons may demand that specific videos be permanently removed from the library. None of these is censorship, although they may well lead to, or reflect, a climate in which censorship is growing.

But a library director or school principal who removes or authorizes the removal of the video *is* censoring. A legislative body that enacts criminal penalties for the display of materials is censoring. They are using the power of government to mandate or enforce ignorance of some material.

Sometimes officials seek not to prohibit or suppress, but merely to restrict access. Usually, this means prohibiting the distribution of various materials or messages to minors. Is this censorship?

I believe it is: Government power is being used to suppress publications on the basis of their content. The Supreme Court may have decided that this is not a violation of the First Amendment. There may be strong social consensus that it is appropriate. You, as an individual, might support it. It is nonetheless official government action, not a decision by private individuals. That's censorship.

What Is a Challenge?

Far more common than censorship, however, is the *challenging* of materials. What is a challenge?

A challenge is a request that a government body or official practice censorship.

So again, parents who exercise their authority to forbid their children from reading something are not censors. Parents who demand that the library remove a movie they don't want their children to see are not censoring. They are merely petitioning a governmental agency—the local library—to undertake censorship on their behalf. They are submitting a challenge, either formally or informally.

Under the First Amendment to the U.S. Constitution, we are free to speak, free to hear, free to write, and free to read. And we are also free to tell anybody who will listen to us how much we despise what we hear and read.

Today's growth of book clubs is the clearest possible demonstration. The liveliest, most interesting, best discussions occur not when everyone nods in satiated contentment, but when readers square off in disagreement about the intent of the book, the moral fiber of the characters, the underlying philosophy of the author, the accuracy of the portrayal of some industry or political situation.

Conflict is at the core of great literature. It is also at the core of our relationship with literature.

What Is Intellectual Freedom?

Historically, libraries have opposed censorship. The two key institutional values of the modern public library are intellectual freedom and patron confidentiality. (I will explore how these developed in "The Library Bill of Rights," later in this chapter.)

What is intellectual freedom?

Intellectual freedom is the belief in the fundamental dignity of individual inquiry and the right to exercise it.

To librarians, whose jobs consist of gathering, organizing, and publicly presenting intellectual capital, inquiry is the defining human characteristic, regardless of age, sex, sexual orientation, race, religion, or politics. Our mission is to make it possible for the public to explore the world of ideas.

In practice, of course, most public libraries in the United States do *not* present the whole world of ideas. We present the mainstream of American publishing. We buy those items for which a few big publishers believe there will be an audience. Thus, much of our collection clusters around what is popular. That may be a particular author—John Grisham or Stephen King. It may be a perennial topic, such as cooking or gardening. It may be a fad: Rubik's cube or the Atkins diet.

Then there are formats and subgenres. We have graphic novels, DVDs, children's literature, and electronic databases, all with their own audiences and issues.

There is also, to a much lesser extent, a gathering of oddball items: small press, alternative, or fringe materials. These are nonetheless important. By definition, the big changes in our society are *not* mainstream. It makes sense to keep an eye on the wilderness.

But library services flow from the belief in intellectual freedom, the attempt to gather a good cross section, a representative sample, of the broad ideas and offerings of our culture.

How They Interact

And in general, that mission is well received in American society. Libraries and librarians are seen as helpful and credible.

By far the bulk of our transactions with the public are both positive and popular. In Colorado, two out of every three citizens have a library card. In my own county, four of every five households use the library regularly; our quarter of a million patrons check out more than four and a half million items each year, and we have hundreds of thousands of other transactions with them. That's the real story of libraries.

Then there are the complaints. Some are happy, if querulous, exchanges between staff and public ("What on earth was that author *thinking?*" "Yes, this is worse than his last one!"). Some are more difficult ("Why are you wasting my taxpayer dollars on this idiotic magazine?"). There is a steady stream of complaints in libraries—as there are in any other public institution.

Then there are the formal challenges, typically from faithful library patrons who were offended by something and really want you to agree with them. Generally speaking, this represents a small percentage of either purchase decisions or the general collection. For instance, I have received more challenges than any library director I know—at this point nearly two hundred in sixteen years. But those two hundred are a tiny percentage of the more than a million items we've purchased in that time.

Finally, there are those cases when, in fact, you agree with the challengers and turn a challenge into an official action, a removal on the basis of content. This, in most libraries, is still relatively rare.

The Constitution and the First Amendment: Foundations of Intellectual Freedom

Libraries' support of intellectual freedom is based on two fundamental documents: the First Amendment to the U.S. Constitution and the Library Bill of Rights. While it is not within the scope of this book to provide a comprehensive history of either, it is important to understand the context in which they were created.

There are two very different ideas of the First Amendment. One is that a prescient, preternaturally wise, and calmly dignified group of founders solemnly and explicitly enshrined precisely those civil rights we now take for granted. Another is the belief often held by conservative Christians that, in the words of James Dobson, founder of Focus on the Family, "to read the Constitution as the charter for a secular state is to misread history.... The Constitution was designed to perpetuate a Christian order" (Kramnick and Moore, 1996).

Both are false.

Against the first, it's clear that many of today's challenges to intellectual freedom would never have occurred to the founders. They may have been wise—some of them, some of the time—but they could not foresee the future. They did not envision the Internet, or talk radio, or labor unions, or thermonuclear devices. Nor were they in perfect agreement.

Nor could they be counted on to practice what they preached consistently.

Against the second, it's clear that the founders worked hard to erect a figurative wall between church and state—a wall that not only sought to keep the government out of religion, but to keep religion well away from the apparatus of state. Over the years, that wall has been preserved in some respects, and eroded in others.

In brief, the U.S. Constitution and the First Amendment were more reactions against despised practices of England, than they were a carefully worked-out system of alternatives.

There was much to despise.

Seditious Libel and Imprimateur

"For hundreds of years," wrote historian Irving Brant, "Englishmen had been fined, whipped, pilloried, imprisoned and had their ears cut off for speech and writings offensive to government or society" (Hentoff 1980).

That's not hyperbole. Indeed, one unhappy printer had one hand chopped off (with a hammer and a cleaver) merely for suggesting that a monarch had made a bad love match.

People who talk about the history of free speech often begin with "prior restraint"—the process through which government forbids the production of writings on a topic. This refers to the English practice, adopted in 1538, of the "imprimateur"—permission from the state, via a license, to publish (Werhan 2004).

The practice lasted more than a hundred years. Following some of the abuses by the English monarchy, the imprimateur was briefly abolished for four years (when the monarchy was itself overthrown), then reinstituted in 1644. In John Milton's "Areopagitica," he addressed the practice: "Give me the liberty to know, to utter, and to argue freely according to conscience, above all liberties." Yet the imprimateur lasted another fifty years after that (Werhan 2004).

Another censorious practice was that of seditious libel. The British common law concept was "notoriously broad." In the seventeenth century, the courts made it worse. They declared that the truth of a statement had no bearing as a defense. Indeed, the courts held that truth was even more pernicious, since it was liable to spread faster and last longer than an outright lie. One might merely point out a problem with a particular government policy, and face fines, imprisonment, or death. As a result, members of Parliament passed a law exempting them from the charge—a historical antecedent preserved in our own Constitution's Article I, section 6, clause 1, which immunizes members of Congress for their "Speech or Debate in either house" (Werhan 2004).

Religious Freedom and the Wall of Separation

Pursuit of Truth

Yet neither the imprimateur nor seditious speech has much endured in the popular mind. Today, Americans are more apt to remember that the colonies were founded by people seeking religious freedom.

In England before the American Revolution, religion was very much a matter of state. There was a long history of religious persecution, the requirement of religious oaths, and a unity, followed by abuse, of religious and political power.

The Test and Corporation Acts (1673), directed at Catholics, required all holders of civil or military offices under the British crown to receive the sacrament according to the rites of the Anglican church.

Nonsubscribers could not run for office. Non-Anglicans could not matriculate from Oxford or Cambridge. The main targets of these laws were Protestants: Baptists, Presbyterians, Independents, Congregationalists, Unitarians, and Quakers.

Many of the fiery speakers of the day sought broad freedom of expression. Often, this concerned the debate over religious questions, in particular, the importance of private conscience over authority.

Once in America, some settlers sought to establish a Christian commonwealth. And here it became clear that freedom was relative. Early colonists perpetuated many of the same institutions that drove them from England: requiring tithes for church support (albeit for more than one church, at least in seven of the original thirteen colonies), instituting mandatory church attendance, and punishing individuals for crimes of heresy.

In short, "The persistent image of colonial America as a society in which freedom of expression was cherished is an hallucination of sentiment that ignores history" (Levy 1985).

But the practice outpaced the official "right" of free speech—no doubt because of the distance from English authority and the difficulty of enforcing orthodoxy across an ocean.

We see in America's first Constitution—the Massachusetts "Body of Liberties" of 1641—some telling provisions. Any community could form its own church, and the state would have nothing to say in the matter. Conversely, churches were expected to keep out of the business of civil government. Censure by a church could not affect a person's civil privileges. One church could have no say in the affairs of another. No one could be forced to attend any specific church. Of particular interest is the fact that ministers could not hold political office (Schweber 2003).

By contrast, consider the words from the Texas Republican Party platform of 2004 (cited at www.theocracywatch.org/texas_gop.htm): "Our Party pledges to exert its influence to restore the original intent of the

First Amendment of the United States Constitution and dispel the myth of the separation of Church and State."

The phrase "separation of church and state" is often attributed to Thomas Jefferson. He used it in his 1802 letter to the Baptist Association of Danbury, Connecticut, where he wrote, "... I contemplate with sovereign reverence that act of the whole American people which declared that their legislature should 'make no law respecting an establishment of religion, or prohibiting the free exercise thereof,' thus building a wall of separation between Church and State" (Schweber 2003)

But the "wall" had been talked about before then. Roger Williams, an outspoken advocate of religious liberty, had fled the Massachusetts Puritans and settled Rhode Island in protest against the extent to which the state was involved in religious matters (this was before the 1641 Constitution). Williams spoke of "a wall of separation between the garden of the Church and the wilderness of the world," and declared that "it is the will and command of God that ... a permission of the most pagan, Jewish, Turkish, or anti-Christian consciences and worships, be granted to all men in all nations and countries." "An enforced uniformity of religion," he wrote, "confounds the civil and religious" (Schweber 2003).

But even before then, a man who was both widely read by, and deeply influential on, the founders had discussed this wall. It was essential to "build an impenetrable wall of separation between things sacred and civil," wrote Scottish dissenting minister and political writer James Burgh. His book *Crito*, published in London 1767, was a response to the British Test and Corporation Acts of 1673.

In their brief but pointed book, *The Godless Constitution: The Case Against Religious Correctness*, authors Isaac Kramnick and R. Laurence Moore (1996) argue persuasively that the Constitution and the First Amendment were "godless by design." Neither God, nor Jesus, appears anywhere in the Constitution. It is clear from the writings of the time, and in particular, by the ratification debates around the Constitution and the Bill of Rights, that the founders knew exactly what they were doing and why.

Jefferson also raised this caution, seldom remembered by today's religious right: "[Political support of religion] tends only to corrupt the principles of that religion it is meant to encourage, by bribing with a monopoly of worldly honours and emoluments, those who will externally profess and conform to it." Political advantage is by nature ever changing. In theory, at least, religion describes the eternal. To Jefferson and others, religion corrupted the state (or as he put it, "The clergy, by getting themselves established by law and ingrafted into the machine of government, have been a very formidable engine against the civil and religious rights of man"). But the state also corrupted religion. Or as James Madison said, "Religion and government will both exist in greater purity, the less they are mixed together" (Schweber 2003).

Another persistent and false idea is that the founders were "born-again Christians." According to Arthur Schlesinger, Jr., "John Adams was a Unitarian, which Trinitarians abhorred as heresy. Thomas Jefferson, denounced as an atheist, was actually a deist who detested organized religion and who produced an expurgated version of the New Testament with the miracles eliminated. Jefferson and James Madison, a nominal Episcopalian, were the architects of the Virginia Statute of Religious Freedom. James Monroe was another Virginia Episcopalian. John Quincy Adams was another Massachusetts Unitarian." George Washington was such a model of precedent and diplomacy, nobody knows what he thought, but his private correspondence never mentions Jesus (cited at www.theocracywatch.org/separation_church_state2.htm, accessed 2006).

Another odd bit of bad history is the idea that the Bible (the Ten Commandments or any other part) somehow forms the basis of common law, either in England or in the United States. It does not.

According to the Constitution's Seventh Amendment: "In suits at common law ... the right of trial by jury shall be preserved; and no fact, tried by a jury, shall be otherwise re-examined in any court of the United States than according to the rules of the common law."

Here, many Christians believe that common law came from Christian foundations and therefore the Constitution derives from it. They use various quotes from Supreme Court justices proclaiming that Christianity came as part of the laws of England, and therefore from its common law heritage.

But Thomas Jefferson elaborated about the history of common law in his letter to Thomas Cooper on February 10, 1814 (Lipscomb and Bergh 1903):

> For we know that the common law is that system of law which was introduced by the Saxons on their settlement in England, and altered from time to time by proper legislative authority from that time to the date of Magna Charta, which terminates the period of the common law.... This settlement took place about the middle of the fifth century. But Christianity was not introduced till the seventh century; the conversion of the first Christian king of the Heptarchy having taken place about the year 598, and that of the last about 686. Here then, was a space of two hundred years, during which the common law was in existence, and Christianity no part of it.
>
> ... if any one chooses to build a doctrine on any law of that period, supposed to have been lost, it is incumbent on him to prove it to have existed, and what were its contents. These were so far alterations of the common law, and became themselves a part of it. But none of these adopt Christianity as a part of the common law. If, therefore, from the settlement of the Saxons to the introduction of Christianity among them, that system of religion could not be a part of the common law, because they were not yet Christians, and if, having their laws from that period to the close of the common law, we are all able to find among them no such act of adoption, we may safely affirm (though

contradicted by all the judges and writers on earth) that Christianity neither is, nor ever was a part of the common law.

In the same letter, Jefferson examined how the error spread about Christianity and common law. Jefferson realized that a misinterpretation had occurred with a Latin term by Prisot, "ancien scripture," in reference to common law history. The term meant "ancient scripture" but people had incorrectly interpreted it to mean "holy scripture," thus spreading the myth that common law came from the Bible. Jefferson writes:

> And Blackstone repeats, in the words of Sir Matthew Hale, that 'Christianity is part of the laws of England,' citing Ventris and Strange ubi surpa. 4. Blackst. 59. Lord Mansfield qualifies it a little by saying that 'The essential principles of revealed religion are part of the common law.' In the case of the Chamberlain of London v. Evans, 1767. But he cites no authority, and leaves us at our peril to find out what, in the opinion of the judge, and according to the measure of his foot or his faith, are those essential principles of revealed religion obligatory on us as a part of the common law.
>
> Thus we find this string of authorities, when examined to the beginning, all hanging on the same hook, a perverted expression of Priscot's, or on one another, or nobody." (Peterson 1994)

The *Encyclopedia Britannica* also describes the Saxon origin and adds: "The nature of the new common law was at first much influenced by the principles of Roman law, but later it developed more and more along independent lines." Also prominent among the characteristics that derived out of common law were the institution of the jury and the right to speedy trial (Walker 1997).

But back to the nature of religion itself. To the founders, "religion appears simultaneously as specially valuable and specially dangerous" (Schweber 2003). It is valuable in that it embodies the pursuit of happiness and meaning, of conscience and liberty. It is dangerous in that it may compromise the liberty of others. And so it remains.

Another factor in the creation of the First Amendment was the belief that only through open debate could the truth be determined.

Sir Francis Bacon, an influential writer and natural philosopher, had defined the project of scientific reason as the dispelling of myths. To the Calvinists, the natural world could be described as the "second book of revelation." Their tradition denied any special authority of priests to interpret either its meaning or that of written scripture (Schweber 2003).

In brief, there was an English tradition of dissenting Protestantism, scientific reasoning, and Enlightenment politics. All of them rejected the imposition of external authority.

James Madison also wrote about the need to examine the evidence independently: "Whilst we assert for ourselves a freedom to embrace, to profess and to observe the Religion which we believe to be of divine origin, we cannot deny an equal freedom to those whose minds have not yet yielded to the evidence which has convinced us" (Schweber 2003).

Jefferson, something of an amateur scientist himself, made a similar distinction. "[O]ur civil rights," he said, "have no dependence on our religious opinions, any more than our opinions in physics or geometry" (Schweber 2003).

One of the many ironies of the history of the First Amendment is this story. Thomas Jefferson, "author of the Declaration of American Independence, of the Statute of Virginia for Religious Freedom and Father of the University of Virginia" (as it says on his gravestone), and just past President of the United States, tried in 1814 to buy an astronomy book through the mail—only to find that various authorities wouldn't let him. He wrote:

> I am really mortified to be told that, in the United States of America, a fact like this [i.e., the purchase of an apparent geological or astronomical work] can become a subject of inquiry, and of criminal inquiry too, as an offense against religion; that a question about the sale of a book can be carried before the civil magistrate. Is this then our freedom of religion? And are we to have a censor whose imprimatur shall say what books may be sold, and what we may buy? And who is thus to dogmatize religious opinions for our citizens? Whose foot is to be the measure to which ours are all to be cut or stretched? Is a priest to be our inquisitor, or shall a layman, simple as ourselves, set up his reason as the rule for what we are to read, and what we must believe? It is an insult to our citizens to question whether they are rational beings or not, and blasphemy against religion to suppose it cannot stand the test of truth and reason. If [this] book be false in its facts, disprove them; if false in its reasoning, refute it. But, for God's sake, let us freely hear both sides, if we choose. (Lipscomb and Bergh 1903–1904)

Adoption and Ratification

There wasn't much debate about the First Amendment at the time of its adoption. Apparently, the only recorded statement in the congressional debate concerning the "speech and press" clauses was in opposition. But the reasoning was surprising: The statement was unnecessary. The government hadn't been granted the right to abridge such speech, so couldn't claim it by default (Werhan 2004).

James Madison, who had introduced the proposed Bill of Rights that very day, responded that freedom of speech was linked with freedom of assembly, as a vital means through which the people communicated with their representatives.

It was essential, Madison argued, to place freedom of speech and the press beyond the reach of any branch of government. Madison declared that the greatest danger to liberty is to be found, "in the body of the people, operating by the majority against the minority" (Werhan 2004).

The Bill of Rights was adopted by the First Congress in 1789. Eventually, it was ratified by the states, but only after several attempts to amend it. A Christian preamble to the Constitution was proposed—and firmly rejected (as it was again during the Civil War, when it was alleged that our godless Constitution, not slavery, was the cause of "our national tragedy and trial"). A religious test—swearing that one was a believer in God, or a Christian, before one could hold public office—was also debated, and roundly defeated (Kramnick and Moore 1996).

On December 15, 1791, the Bill of Rights became the first ten amendments to the Constitution.

The final version of the First Amendment read as follows: "Congress shall make no law respecting an establishment of religion, or prohibiting the free exercise thereof; or abridging the freedom of speech, or of the press; or the right of the people peaceably to assemble, and to petition the government for a redress of grievances."

And there was to be no religious test for public office. Article VI, clause 3 of our Constitution states "... no religious Test shall ever be required as a Qualification to any Office or public Trust under the United States."

A New Nation: The Alien and Sedition Acts

Then, of course, the wisdom of the founders was universally hailed, and the system was simply applied, without contradiction or controversy.

No.

As Werhan notes, "As would be true of so much of the Constitution, the meaning of freedom of speech, of necessity, would be worked out in the course of the American experiment in constitutional self-government."

Just seven years later, the First Amendment was severely tested. Dominated by the Federalist Party, the 1798 Congress enacted the Alien and Sedition Acts, "making political dissent against government policy as dangerous as if there were no First Amendment in the new republic" (Hentoff 1980).

The reasons were twofold. First, the United States was under threat of war with France, and the act allowed the rounding up and deportation of spies. Second, the Federalists wanted to stifle the political power of the Republicans, led by Thomas Jefferson, who had narrowly lost the presidency to John Adams.

Twenty-five men, most of them editors of Republican newspapers, and one of them the grandson of Benjamin Franklin, were arrested. Their newspapers were shut down.

If charged under the acts, one was permitted to use, as a defense, the truth of an allegedly libelous claim about the government. There was no prior restraint on what might be published. But people could be punished afterwards—a distinction James Madison called "a mockery" (Werhan 2004). In fact, the Alien and Sedition Acts angered many of the founders.

The law came to an abrupt end at the termination of John Adams's presidency. Among his first actions, Jefferson pardoned all who had been found guilty under the acts (although there were not many), and directed that their fines should be repaid.

Civil War

The next significant challenge to the First Amendment came in the conflict leading up to, and during, the Civil War.

In *Barron v. Baltimore,* a case having nothing to do with the First Amendment, the Supreme Court asserted that the Bill of Rights restricted only the actions of the federal government. It did not apply to the states. Clearly, this had implications for free speech.

Not long afterward, North Carolina outlawed the circulation of material sent south by abolitionists. Although most slaves couldn't read, and in fact, much of this material was intended to persuade slaveholders to change their ways, North Carolina feared it would "cause slaves to become discontented with the bondage in which they are held by their masters and the laws regulating the same, and free negroes to be dissatisfied with their social condition and the denial to them of political privileges, and thereby to excite among the said slaves and free negroes a disposition to make conspiracies, insurrections, or resistance" (Werhan 2004).

By 1836, northern congressmen started attaching antislavery provisions to unrelated bills—much as today's congressional representatives attach antiabortion provisions. The topic grew so divisive that Congress adopted a rule that barred even the discussion of abolition in the House and Senate.

In the southern Illinois town of Alton, Elijah P. Lovejoy, a Presbyterian minister and abolitionist editor, became a free speech martyr. First, mobs destroyed three of his printing presses. He asked for the protection of local authorities and was denied. He succeeded, with a group of supporters, in holding off a fourth attack. When another mob tried to set fire to the warehouse where he'd hidden the press, Lovejoy was shot and killed.

It was not an isolated incident; other abolitionist printers faced similar violence. But Lovejoy was something like the civil rights activists of the 1960s—his death captured the popular imagination and produced a remarkably swift transformation of public opinion.

By 1850s, the new antislavery Republican Party put free expression at the core of its agenda.

Once the Civil War began, there were a host of new restrictions on civil liberties. *Habeas corpus* was suspended. Free speech was clamped down on. Lincoln claimed that he tried to permit expression that threatened "the political prospects of the administration," and took aim only at those whose antiwar speech discouraged enlistment into the army or encouraged desertion. But there were many excesses.

By the conclusion of the Civil War, the Fourteenth Amendment guaranteed due process to all naturally born or naturalized citizens, and stated that all were due the "equal protection of the laws." But as late as 1873, the Supreme Court was creating exemptions to the application of federal laws by distinguishing between federal and state rights.

It wasn't until 1925, in *Gitlow v. New York*, that the Supreme Court finally embraced what would seem to have been established long before: the guarantee of all constitutional and amendment rights to the actions of state governments. This decision marks for many historians the beginning of modern law.

A Theory of the First Amendment

Since 1925, there have been many Supreme Court cases involving various First Amendment issues. It's a subject worthy of its own book. Indeed, many excellent sources are available. But other than adjudications around obscenity, children, and the Internet (which I will take up separately), few directly apply to libraries and are beyond the scope of this work.

What then, can we conclude about the First Amendment?

In a 1965 article, Thomas I. Emerson attempted to lay out a theory of the First Amendment. What were its themes?

He concluded, in brief, that there were four:

Maintenance of a system of free expression is necessary

(1) as assuring individual self-fulfillment,

(2) as a means of attaining the truth,

(3) as a method of securing participation by the members of the society in social, including political, decision-making, and

(4) as maintaining the balance between stability and change in the society. (Schweber 2003)

The first of these we have considered, in part, as a matter of religious expression. The First Amendment allows for speaking freely about matters of conscience, and the freedom from compulsion to act contrary to that conscience in religious matters, or other matters of strong belief.

The second idea has also been addressed. The Supreme Court has clearly upheld that the best response to bad speech is better speech, not silence.

The third idea seems to me to be the overarching theme of the First Amendment, and continues to be true even since Emerson's article. A significant purpose of the First Amendment is to advance the equality of all individuals in our society, specifically through the ability to speak and advocate for various perspectives. This is the direct outgrowth of the 1925 Supreme Court decision to fully implement the Fourteenth Amendment, which is itself a fulfillment of the promise inherent in the Declaration of Independence.

The fourth idea is an important one—a restriction on the absolutist interpretation of free speech. The Supreme Court has ruled that there are indeed many restrictions on the right of individuals to express themselves. There are legitimate purposes of the state and its institutions, necessary for governance. Under the First Amendment, you can't burn your draft card because this government document had purposes the Supreme Court judged of importance for the order of the state. (You can burn a photocopy.) You can't use people's mailboxes to deliver your own messages. That's reserved for the post office. You can't usurp the operation of an institution simply to make a point, unless that institution has become a public forum, where your views can be made. You can't shout "fire" in a crowded theater. You can't make big, outrageous, malicious lies that injure people's reputations (although the more public the subject of your lies is, the more you can get away with).

In short, the Supreme Court does give preference to First Amendment rights. The First Amendment enjoys a privileged status. But those rights are not absolute. They are part of a larger social framework, against which they may come into conflict and thus require thoughtful judgment to balance.

The Library Bill of Rights

The second foundational document upon which library support for intellectual freedom rests is the Library Bill of Rights.

The History of the Library Bill of Rights

This document, now central to an understanding of modern librarianship, was not always with us. At the beginning of our profession, our early selection tools and recommended bibliographies were decidedly prescriptive. Less mainstream, more controversial works—Theodore Dreiser's *Sister Carrie*, Eleanor Glyn's *Three Weeks*, Thomas Hardy's *Tess of the D'Urbervilles*, George Bernard Shaw's *Man and Superman*, and Mark Twain's *The Adventures of Huckleberry Finn* and *Tom Sawyer*, "were excluded from key bibliographies and library collections, at least until the literary establishment accepted them as part of the canon" (Samek 2001). Moreover, many librarians saw their role as improving society, through the exposure of citizens to great literature, a decidedly nonpopulist stance (Samek 2001).

From 1876 through about 1939, American libraries went through a profound shift in attitude. (See *Forbidden Books in American Public Libraries, 1876–1939: A Study in Cultural Change* by Evelyn Geller.) In brief, at first we strove to present only what was approved, and disdained what was not. By the early days of World War I, libraries were cooperating in prohibiting access to subversive materials and promoting nationalist propaganda.

At the same time, according to Judith Krug (Office for Intellectual Freedom 2002), "John Steinbeck's *The Grapes of Wrath* became the target of censorship pressures around the country. It was banned from libraries in East St. Louis, Illinois; Camden, New Jersey; Bakersfield, California; and other localities. While some objected to the 'immorality' of the work, most opposed the social views advanced by the author."

On November 21, 1938, the Des Moines Public Library adopted a statement created by library director Forrest Spaulding. It began, "Now when indications in many parts of the world point to growing intolerance, suppression of free speech, and censorship, affecting the rights of minorities and individuals, the Board of Trustees of the Des Moines Public Library reaffirms these basic policies governing a free public library ..."

By 1939, with minor changes, this became the American Library Association's (ALA) "Library's Bill of Rights," our profession's "basic policy statement on intellectual freedom involving library materials" (Office for Intellectual Freedom 2002).

It proved the seed for a potent transformation. By 1940, ALA had established what is now known as the Intellectual Freedom Committee (IFC). Since then, Krug writes, "its main function has been to recommend policies concerning intellectual freedom ..."

The language of the original Library Bill of Rights focused on book selection, a balanced collection, and open meeting rooms. Over time, that changed.

- In 1944, language was introduced (after challenges concerning a book about interracial love) to defend works that were "factually correct." This language was later removed when a Catholic claimed that a work by a Protestant "lacked sound factual authority." Clearly, libraries can't vet, or even review, all the claims a book might make, particularly those of a supernatural nature.

- By 1948, language was added recognizing the need of libraries to challenge "censorship of books urged or practiced by volunteer arbiters of morals or political opinion or by organizations that would establish a coercive concept of Americanism."

- Also in 1948, a new Article IV recognized the need of libraries to cooperate with "allied groups ... in science, education, and book publishing in resisting all abridgment of the free access to ideas and full freedom of expression." Together with resistance to censorship, the Library Bill of Rights clearly calls out an activist approach to intellectual freedom.

- Another 1948 revision added "art" to the provision of public meeting space and exhibits.

- In 1951, language was added to include nonprint materials in library collections, following attacks against films allegedly promoting communism.

- In 1967, following civil rights activism, the document warned against excluding materials because of the social views of an author.
- In 1967, meetings were made "open to the public."
- In 1980, this succinct statement was introduced: "Materials should not be excluded because of the origin, background, or views of those contributing to their creation."

On January 23, 1980, the ALA council adopted the recommendations of the IFC and established the present-day Library Bill of Rights.

The Library Bill of Rights: Final Version

The American Library Association affirms that all libraries are forums for information and ideas, and that the following basic policies should guide their services.

  I. Books and other library resources should be provided for the interest, information, and enlightenment of all people of the community the library serves. Materials should not be excluded because of the origin, background, or views of those contributing to their creation.

  II. Libraries should provide materials and information presenting all points of view on current and historical issues. Materials should not be proscribed or removed because of partisan or doctrinal disapproval.

  III. Libraries should challenge censorship in the fulfillment of their responsibility to provide information and enlightenment.

  IV. Libraries should cooperate with all persons and groups concerned with resisting abridgment of free expression and free access to ideas.

  V. A person's right to use a library should not be denied or abridged because of origin, age, background, or views.

  VI. Libraries which make exhibit spaces and meeting rooms available to the public they serve should make such facilities available on an equitable basis, regardless of the beliefs or affiliations of individuals or groups requesting their use.

Adopted June 18, 1948, by the ALA Council; amended February 2, 1961; January 23, 1980; inclusion of "age" reaffirmed January 23, 1996.

Interpretations

The First Amendment has just 45 words. Its interpretations run to thousands of pages of court documents. The Library Bill of Rights has 191 words. Its interpretations are documents that are typically developed by the IFC, then approved by the ALA council. These interpretations tend to be relatively short—one or two typeset pages.

The practice of adopting interpretations, rather than amending the Library Bill of Rights, was done for two important reasons. First, a document that is frequently revised to reflect current terms or targets of discrimination also frequently becomes dated. It risks becoming a laundry list that inevitably leaves something out, thereby exposing what has not been named to implicit rejection. It was thought better to write the document more broadly and issue interpretations as needed.

The second reason is more subtle. In 1993, ALA's mid-winter meeting was held in Colorado, just three months after the state had adopted Amendment 2, a state constitutional amendment repealing various civil rights protections for gays and lesbians. In protest, the IFC proposed amending the Library Bill of Rights to identify gays and lesbians for specific inclusion as people whose rights should not be abridged.

But the "laundry list" concern remained. There was also something new: Various groups around the country (specifically, a Virginia-based organization called Family Friendly Libraries) had sprung up. This group specifically targeted the Library Bill of Rights and had sought its repeal or revision at the local library level. For ALA to add demonstrably divisive language to the Library Bill of Rights at that point in history and force local libraries to re-adopt that language might well have provided an opening for its complete rejection.

Instead, an interpretation was crafted that merely clarified the Library Bill of Rights, explaining that gays and lesbians were already included, that they had not been excluded from the Library Bill of Right's clearly broad language. Again, this is precisely what happens when the Supreme Court finds something in the First Amendment that had not been called out before—a right to privacy, for instance.

Since 1988, there have been four interpretations:

1. **1988:** The "Universal Right to Free Expression" (addressing the barrier of language) and "Economic Barriers to Information Access"
2. **1989:** "Access for Children and Young People to Videotapes and Other Nonprint Formats"
3. **1993:** "Access to Library Resources and Services Regardless of Gender or Sexual Orientation"
4. **1996:** "Access to Electronic Information, Services, and Networks" and a Q & A in 1997

Its Significance

What is the significance of the Library Bill of Rights? I believe there are three.

First, it establishes a core purpose for the public library, a distinct, definable mission in American society. We provide "books and other library resources for the interest, information, and enlightenment of all people of the community the library serves."

Second, it parallels the developmental arc of the First Amendment. That is, its foundational principles reach for ever-greater inclusiveness and equality of individual access. Where the First Amendment sought equal access to the law, the Library Bill of Rights sought equal access to library materials and services. Even the issue of patron confidentiality—another profoundly important principle, and a second foundational pillar of the meaning of public libraries in our nation—is clearly derived from the Library Bill of Rights. After all, one does not have the freedom to read and write without the privacy to do so.

Third, as noted below (see the chapter entitled "Responding to Challenges"), the Library Bill of Rights, and various interpretations, are crucial in responding to citizen complaints. They are important tools in educating a lay board in the essential principles of librarianship. They also let the public know that the lay board has reviewed and discussed those principles—and knows what the institution stands for.

More specifically, my discussions with thousands of librarians have clearly demonstrated a plain fact: Censorship occurs most often, and most successfully, in those libraries that have not taken the trouble to adopt essential policies and procedures. Such policies begin with the Library Bill of Rights. They do not end there. **Libraries that operate without a Materials Selection Policy, or a clearly defined Reconsideration Policy, will have items withdrawn—and have very little recourse.** Libraries without such policies are like jewelry stores that leave their doors open all night; they are going to get hit.

Incidentally, such policies are not hard to come by. Most state library associations now offer an online "Intellectual Freedom Handbook" with sample language. In Colorado, it can be found at www.cal-webs.org/ifhandbook.html.

But What about the Children?

When I give presentations on this topic, I describe a common situation. Suppose I have a young son who sasses me (I do have a son, but he's not so young anymore, and I wouldn't calling it "sassing.") Here are my options:

1. Put him in a timeout, whether that be confinement to a bedroom, standing in a corner, or in a closet.
2. Send him to bed without supper.
3. Spank or slap him.

Is there any other group in America whose free speech may be legally responded to by incarceration, starvation, and corporal punishment?

Do children have free speech rights? Do they have a right to information?

In brief, the answer is just barely. There are a handful of court cases. Books, already purchased, may not be pulled from a school library solely on the basis of content. Teens can wear black armbands in protest of a war. They seem to have some free press rights—as with a student newspaper. But all of these are limited by various other rights of the adults who look after them.

Obscenity

Of particular interest to librarians—primarily because so many books and films in the United States have faced the charge—is the idea of "obscenity."

Obscenity doesn't make much of an appearance in the early history of free speech. People were too busy fighting over politics and religion.

Our legal concern with obscenity really began with Anthony Comstock. A devout Christian, he adopted the fight against prostitution and immorality in the late 1860s, then headed to Washington, D.C., to get the nation's first anti-obscenity law passed in 1873. He was rewarded with an unpaid postal inspector position, which he used with vigor to promote his cause. He is alleged to have boasted about the number of "libertines" that he had driven to suicide. He was particularly exercised about the distribution of birth control information. In 1914, birth control activist Margaret Sanger was prosecuted under the Comstock Act. Comstock was even in the audience.

However, the Supreme Court didn't address the issue of obscenity until the twentieth century. It was time. Between 1934 and 1957, obscenity charges were brought against James Joyce's *Ulysses;* Radclyffe Hall's *The Well of Loneliness;* Henry Miller's *Tropic of Cancer* and *Tropic of Capricorn;* a songbook called *Give Out: Songs of, for, and by the Men in the Service;* William Faulkner's *Mosquitoes; The Complete Book of Birth Control;* Ernest Hemingway's *To Have and Have Not;* and others.

Finally, in 1957, the case of *Roth v. United States* gave the first definitive Supreme Court response. In brief, it upheld the Comstock Act.

There are many internal contradictions about this subject, reflecting the country's schizophrenia about sex. For instance, in 1969, the Supreme Court declared that individuals had the right to read or view sexual materials in private. However, in 1971, it also decided that the state and federal governments could continue to prohibit its sale, mailing, or other distribution. In other words, you could have it, but you couldn't get it.

In 1970, the Presidential Commission of Obscenity and Pornography (appointed by Lyndon Johnson) made its report to Richard Nixon. Its exhaustive review of available evidence led to a few recommendations, including eliminating censorship for consenting adults across the board, but continuing it for juveniles. "Without taking the time to study the report or to consult the technical data upon which its conclusions were built, the U.S. Senate, with only five members in dissent, voted to condemn it" (Tedford 1997). President Nixon noted grimly that "American morality is not to be trifled with," and totally rejected the report. Moreover, he set about appointing judges to reverse the "libertine" and "liberal" tendencies of the times.

This stood until *Miller v. California* in 1973, when the court defined obscene materials according to a three-part test:

1. The average person (not a child), "applying contemporary community standards" would find the work, taken as a whole, appeals to the prurient interest.
2. The work depicts or describes, in a patently offensive way, sexual conduct specifically defined by the applicable state law.
3. The work, taken as a whole, lacks serious literary, artistic, political, or scientific value. This last is known as the SLAPS test.

As Kathleen Sullivan (now dean of Stanford Law School) has said, "The first two parts of the Miller test are incoherent: To put it crudely, they require the audience to be turned on and grossed out at the same time" (Office for Intellectual Freedom 2002).

The third test has a twist to it, too. Nixon succeeded in appointing an unprecedented four new judges to the Supreme Court. At least five obscenity cases were held up until the new Court was filled. The Court then decided that government prosecutors are under no obligation to present expert testimony from the literary, artistic, political, or scientific communities. Rather, prosecutors need only show the materials to the jury. As Tedford notes, "This ruling has the effect of shifting the primary burden of proof to the accused, who now bears the responsibility of trying to demonstrate that the materials do have serious value." The accused are guilty until proven innocent.

Tedford summarizes the obscenity debate as follows: "In the United States, obscenity is the last religio-moral heresy to be suppressed by government authority on behalf of the nation's majority religion." This, of course, raises questions about the establishment of religion.

But the Supreme Court decisions are instructive in several respects. The Court changes its membership, changes its interpretations, and thus changes the law. It's a moving target. Nothing is settled.

In Loco Parentis

The Latin phrase *in loco parentis* means "the parents are crazy." OK, not really. It means "in the position or place of a parent," or acting in the stead of a parent. For instance, when you drop off your child at a public school, the school takes temporary custody of the child. It operates *in loco parentis.*

This is in stark contrast to the public library. After many discussions during the 1960s, it was generally concluded that the public library does *not* serve in place of parents. To put it another way, "the parents, not the library, are responsible for their children's use of the Internet" (American Library Association 2001)

This is precisely what irks many library critics. Despite their general rejection of government or institutional authority, organizations such as Family Friendly Libraries want the public library to act as parents, restricting access to information and enforcing their values for all children.

Children and the Internet: Definitions

As Mike Godwin, staff counsel for the Electronic Frontier Foundation, wrote in "Kids, Cyberporn, and Hysteria," "When talking about pornography and child safety on the Net, one often sees several different terms bandied about as if they were interchangeable. They're not" (http://www.eff.org/pub/Censorship/kids_and_cyberporn_godwin.article).

Some of those terms are important. Godwin defines pornography as "material that presents sexual content of some sort, with the intent of being arousing." By itself, pornography is not illegal. If it were, every advertiser and filmmaker in the United States would be out of a job.

- **Obscenity.** Pornography that meets all parts of a three-part test, as described above.
- **Child pornography.** As Godwin states bluntly, "This is material that is illegal regardless of whether it is obscene.... Under federal law, 'child pornography' is any visual material that depicts a child either engaging in explicit sexual acts or posing in a 'lewd and lascivious' manner, when the manufacture of such material involves the actual use of a real child."
- **Child sexual abuse**. It's illegal, whether or not there's a picture.
- **Indecency.** To date, this term has been restricted solely to broadcasting and so-called dial-a-porn services, "both currently under the jurisdiction of the Federal Communications Commission. In those contexts, 'indecency' normally means 'patently offensive' sexual content or profane language." Outside of these narrow areas, however, "indecency" has no legal meaning.

Nonetheless, many people believe they know it when they see it. They just don't agree with each other on a consistent basis.

Disagreements notwithstanding, when parents do decide that something is indecent, they tend to steer their own children away from it. The library community isn't eager to put itself between parents and their children. In fact, we would like both parents and children to feel comfortable in our buildings and before our terminals—providing, that is, we don't have to sacrifice the fundamental principles upon which libraries are based.

CPPA, COPA, and CIPA

When you start to encounter a jumble of acronyms, you know there's trouble brewing. As noted in the ALA web page (www.ala.org/ala/oif/ifissues/issuesrelatedlinks/cppacopacipa.htm), there have been a number of federal attempts to address the issue of children and the Internet.

All of them have sought to restrict what is available to minors; all have been challenged by the ALA. As noted earlier, Supreme Court decisions change. But at this writing, here's where we stand: The Supreme Court has upheld the constitutionality of Internet filtering (through the use of various software "protections") for children, and specifically, of the requirement by the federal government that public libraries must filter their terminals if they wish to receive federal funds.

The Child Pornography Prevention Act (CPPA) was an attempt to expand the definition of child pornography. A key provision was to include "virtual" children—those who have been digitally created. The law was struck down as unconstitutional for two reasons. First, it was found to be overly broad. Second, although child pornography is indeed illegal, this is because children are sexually abused in its production. If computer technology is used, or photographs are taken of adults pretending to be minors, the Supreme Court found no basis for a ban. According to ALA, "the Child Pornography Prevention Act affected only those who create films and images. It did not affect libraries."

The Child Online Protection Act (COPA) was an attempt to replace the Communications Decency Act, which was found wholly unconstitutional. "COPA prohibits the transmission of any material over the Internet deemed 'harmful to minors,' if the communication was made for a commercial purpose." This act appears to be in limbo. It was found unconstitutional by the Third Court Circuit of Appeals; that finding was overturned by the Supreme Court. "All nine justices agreed that the injunction preventing any enforcement of COPA must remain in place while the lower courts further examine COPA's constitutionality" (American Library Association 2001).

The Children's Internet Protection Act (CIPA) mandated software filtering for those libraries receiving federal funds.

As the Office of Intellectual Freedom puts it, "The Children's Internet Protection Act (CIPA) designates federal funding for libraries that install filters on all its computers. Libraries that do not accept federal funding do not have to install filters. That is, the Supreme Court's opinion has no effect on libraries that are not covered by CIPA (i.e., libraries that do not receive e-rate discounts or LSTA funds for the provision of public Internet access)."

Of course, there are a host of other state laws, some of which are even more restrictive, mandating filtering without offering any funding, and thereby requiring unreimbursed expenditures. These laws, too, are in flux, and will not be summarized here.

The future of Internet filtering is uncertain. While most of the focus has thus far been on children, the Supreme Court has made it clear that adults may ask to have filtering turned off, in which case libraries must comply. Do adults have the right to watch explicit pornography or extreme graphic violence on public library workstations? Or would the "time and place" restrictions on free speech, or general policies, be sufficient to prevent the viewing of such content in a public place? We don't know, but we do have some bad examples on both sides of the debate.

Some libraries have had full-time content monitors patrolling the Internet area, which is both intrusive and humiliating. Others have adopted such a hands-off attitude that they found themselves with significant public relations problems. An example of the latter is Minneapolis Public Library, which in the late 1990s found that many homeless men were pulling up very graphic images. Women and children complained, but nothing changed, so some stopped coming to the downtown library. Eventually, the local TV station filmed some 50 percent of the Internet stations being used for the display of sexual content. Clearly, some middle ground is desirable if the library is to be useful to all of its constituents.

A Brief History of Technology to the World Wide Web

The Internet has unquestionably expanded the information available to children—and to everyone else with access.

But that's what technology does. Consider the effect of these technologies:

- **Print:** Whether it's newspaper, magazine, or book, print media captures and presents experience, so even those in rural or remote areas can stay current about international events. Teenage boys can sneak peeks at their fathers' *Playboy*. Impressionable young women can read *Sister Carrie*.

- **Automobile:** Once upon a time teenagers and young people, especially in rural areas, couldn't get into too much trouble in a day (or so their parents imagined), because there was only so far they could get by walking, riding a bike, or using a horse and buggy. Enter the automobile—perhaps the most profound influence on America's mating and dating patterns in the modern age. Now sixteen-year-olds can travel three hundred miles or so in an afternoon, limited only by their ability to pay for gas.

- **Radio:** I've spoken to people whose first encounter with a person of color was over the radio. That particular show—*Amos 'n' Andy*—actually involved white actors mimicking what they thought was African American dialect. The radio broadcast "War of the Worlds," predicated on H.G. Wells's story of a Martian invasion, panicked thousands. Generations listened to fireside chats, or *Radio America*, getting swept up in worldwide events, both real and imaginary.

- **Movies:** Movies must join the automobile in their profound effect on American romance. Aside even from mainstream fare, there were many introductions to new social phenomena. *Guess Who's Coming to Dinner?* raised the prospect of interracial marriage. *Rebel Without a Cause* recruited sullen biker wannabes.
- **Television:** Despite Ed Sullivan's attempts to keep the camera away from Elvis Presley's gyrating hips, TV nonetheless delivered him to millions of living rooms. From there it was only a short hop to *Sex and the City*.

The World Wide Web is clearly continuing this tradition. Any technology that allows people or ideas to move quickly from one place to another increases exposure to human experience. To some, that exposure is itself threatening.

Often, then, we will see a flurry of activity when the legislature takes note of the changing times. A recent example might be the V-chip. By Federal Communications Commission mandate the chip was installed into millions of TV sets (half of all new models thirteen inches or larger manufactured after July 1, 1999, and all sets thirteen inches or larger manufactured after January 1, 2000), but it's used by almost no one.

Half a generation later, those roadblocks to change are largely ignored. By then, the perils of the media have been incorporated into more modern life. And we're worrying about the next change.

CHAPTER 2

Religion and Libraries

Most Americans know very little about the history and the influence of religion in this country. In large part, as detailed in *What Johnny Shouldn't Read: Textbook Censorship in America* by Joan DelFattore (1992), this is because that history has been excised from our schools.

No, it's not a liberal plot. It probably had more to do with the work of Mel and Norma Gabler, educational research analysts. Until his death in December 2004, Mel Gabler, a Texas Christian, was a textbook activist. In particular, he scrutinized the big primary and secondary textbook companies' offerings to ensure that they met his strict standards of accuracy. To him and his many followers, that meant that evolution was presented as still disputed, sexual abstinence was taught as a foundation to health instruction, and various Christian and patriotic sentiments were either positively expressed or, at least, not contradicted.

Various court actions have established that publishers have the right to publish history and science information, whether or not it meets with evangelical approval. But Texas is one of two markets deemed essential to the success of a textbook (the other is California). Textbook publishers haven't quite caved in to this pressure. But they haven't demonstrated much courage either. Instead, they've remained silent or been so deliberately vague that they do not offend, but neither do they inform.

The people of the United States have had two persistent fascinations throughout our history: religion and sex. Of the two, we probably do a better job of educating our children about sex.

This chapter explores some of the influences of religion on the use and evaluation of the public library.

Most of what I have learned about responding to challenges has come from four discrete experiences. All of them involved a significant interaction with religion, whether the private faith of a citizen or a more organized action of a church or religious association.

The first was my witnessing of a challenge to a school library in Windsor, Colorado, in 1988 and 1989. It concerned a book called *Big 16*.

The second was a close encounter with Madonna in 1992, concerning her book, *Sex*.

The third was my experience with two religious groups: Focus on the Family (FOF), starting in 1992, and the Church of Jesus Christ of Latter-Day Saints (LDS), or the Mormons, starting in 1994. The contrast between these two institutions is illuminating.

The fourth were formal challenges from the public. I will take that issue up in the chapter entitled "Responding to Challenges."

Big 16

I was the administrator of the Greeley Public Library in Colorado. A woman from Windsor, a rural town to the north, got upset when her first-grader brought home a book from the school library called *Big 16*, by Mary Calhoun.

Big 16 was a Paul Bunyan-esque slave. The number 16 was his shoe size. He was very strong, once fetching back two stray cattle, one under each arm. Eventually, at the request of his twinkly-eyed master—a sort of Colonel Sanders who had been shrunk in the wash—Big 16 actually killed the devil. After his own death, however, Big 16 was denied a place in both heaven and hell. The keepers of the gates—also portrayed as black—feared Big 16's strength. At the story's end, the ghost of Big 16 was wandering through the mist of the South, looking for a home and carrying a flickering lantern.

Big 16 falls into the category of "explaining stories." Why are there flickering lights in the mists of the bayou? Big 16 is looking for a home. I find the book evocative, and ultimately, about the southern white man's fear of the black man.

What was the mother's objection? She didn't think the word "hell" should appear in a book available for use by someone so young.

So the mother did a sensible thing. She went to the local school library and tried to talk with the librarians. She told them that she was not a well-educated woman, but she was a woman of strong faith, and she felt uncomfortable with her son bringing such a book home.

The two librarians were also smart and professional, and they probably did not mean for their approach to be harsh. But as many librarians do when faced with somebody complaining about a book, they huddled together and began speaking the special language of trained librarians, thick with formal references to policies.

They communicated to the woman that such a request was censorship. They provided copies of the relevant policies, and told her that she would have to make a formal request to remove the book.

The woman was hurt and frustrated. But she did make a formal complaint to the school board, in writing. She showed up at a board meeting. There, the complaint was read, and all but sneered at. People actually laughed at her. The book was retained.

However, she had found an ally in the minister of her church. He, too, found the book blasphemous, and stood with her.

The case began to get a little press.

Then she did something unexpected. She met with the Rainbow Coalition in a nearby university town. This book, she told them, is racist. The town she came from had no black people at all. Was it right that the first black person her son encountered, via literature, should be a willing slave?

The members of the Rainbow Coalition were incensed. They called the town "monochromatic." (It was an epithet I found oddly delightful, however inaccurate—in fact the town had a large, and largely ignored, Hispanic population).

The Rainbow Coalition professors called the book a breeding ground for racism and the perpetuation of destructive stereotypes. They wanted that book out of that library.

I got hold of a copy of the original complaint (which was, after all, a public document), and passed it around at a meeting of the group. One Rainbow Coalitionist said, in a shocked and aggrieved tone, "You mean this is a fundamentalist complaint? But that's censorship!" They dropped it.

Lesson one: Censorship is what the *other* side wants to silence.

Then the woman went back to the school library and asked if it would be all right if she just came to school during library hour to help her son find books that she deemed acceptable?

Permission was given, but then, for a variety of innocent reasons, the library hour got moved around unpredictably. On several occasions, when the mother showed up, her son had already been to the library.

What happened next? The woman got tired of the mockery and active interference with what she saw as her right and responsibility to educate her child in accordance with her own values. She pulled the boy from public school.

And where did she go for curricular materials? She came to the public library. My library.

Although she spent a lot of time there with her son, who was thrilled by her presence and their time together, it was a long time before she could bring herself to open up to another librarian. She believed she'd discovered a hard little knot of hypocrisy in our profession. I think she did, too.

When she walked through my library's doors, my first reaction was shame. I believed then, as I do now, that we treated her poorly. I did my best to make it up to her.

The best response to criticism of library practice is not the public humiliation of your accusers. It is the provision of service that both of you can be proud of.

Madonna

For Sex . . . *See Librarian*

In fall of 1992, and with the free, enthusiastic support of the media, Madonna began hawking her latest venture, *Sex*. It came in a heavy mylar wrapping, had a sticker on it reading, "Warning! Adults only!" and at some Denver-area bookstores, was sold only to people over 18 years old. The price was $49.95.

By the time the book came out, our staff had already decided not to purchase it. It was expensive, had an awkward format, had received generally negative reviews, and nobody in our community had requested it.

Then came this article, on the front page of the *Denver Post*, October 22, 1992: "Check out Madonna at Your Library!" The book was or would be available, according to the *Post*, in several metro locations, especially Denver and Boulder.

This came, incidentally, after about thirty Denver-area newspaper plugs in the previous seven days. Interestingly, although the *Post* panned the book and pooh-poohed the suggestion that anyone could take it seriously, they didn't show any of the photographs either, or at least any that might have generated subscriber or advertiser complaints.

At any rate, after the story, I received three requests for the book and twelve protests, all in the same morning. Most of the protests were an organized effort from the members of one church in the Parker area.

The Process

All this generated a lot of very stimulating discussion among our staff. After talking to a number of people around the community, I put the issue before our seven-member Collection Development Committee, which consisted of branch managers and reference staff.

Our internal policy, then set by me, called for us to buy almost anything a patron requested, except those items that were prohibitively expensive or whose subject matter was highly obscure or technical. Madonna's book was certainly pricey, but all of us admitted that we ourselves were curious to see it. Certainly, we had purchased expensive books before.

But did we have a need for this book? Judged on its own merits, we didn't think so.

So then we went to the next question: How many public requests does it take to justify buying an expensive book of little apparent value to our relatively small collection?

Opinions were divided, although the best line of the day was from our business manager: "If you have to be over eighteen, the district can't buy it. We're only two years old." (Our library had converted from a county department to an independent library district in 1990.)

My staff thoroughly discussed the relevant issues. Does sexually explicit material in and of itself pose some kind of threat, moral or otherwise, to the public? Unlikely. Was Madonna a mainstream cultural figure who generates strong public interest? Unquestionably. Would the purchase of the book cause the library some political or funding damage? We decided that it certainly could—but that had never stopped us before nor has it since.

Even if we did buy the book, would the library be able to hang on to it? Probably not. Were we setting a dangerous precedent if we didn't buy the book? It depended on our reasons and how we justified the decision to our community.

I asked for a show of hands. Four staff members thought we should get it. Three thought we shouldn't.

It occurred to me that when we receive written patron requests to remove library materials the first question we ask is, "Did you read the whole book?" None of us had even seen *Sex*.

So I decided to take a look at it. I drove up to a nearby Barnes and Noble bookstore, which had a copy available for perusal by the (adult) public. I had to stand at the counter to examine it, which took about fifteen minutes.

When I asked about the book, a woman standing nearby overheard my request and said she would like to see it, too. So we thumbed through it together and talked about it.

Now let's back up for a moment. Most people quite reasonably expect a public library to carry a broad variety of materials reflecting the many crosscurrents of mainstream culture.

"Mainstream" doesn't mean materials that steer clear of sex. Many, many commonly available titles, from best-sellers to grocery store magazines to blockbuster videos, have quite a lot of sex in them.

You will find such items in our libraries, and I believe they belong there. These materials reflect the increasing cultural tolerance of human sexuality in all of its flavors. On the whole, I think that's a healthy development.

Then there are the kind of materials you probably would not expect public libraries to carry. I'm talking about books with titles like *The Nympho Slave Vixens of Venus*, magazines such as *Jugs*, or videos like *Debbie Does Dallas*. We don't buy those at our library, and I don't know any public library that does.

Somewhere in the middle are magazines such as *Playboy* (indexed by most periodical guides and carried by most larger libraries, although not us at present) and *Penthouse*.

After a lot of careful thinking, I came to the conclusion that *Sex* falls well on the other side of the line from *Playboy*. I think Madonna's book, by her conscious intent, fit the commonly held definition of pornography.

Community Standards

Pornography is a loaded word, of course. But to my mind, it refers primarily to format and to the target market. I don't find pornography necessarily offensive, and I don't use the term pejoratively. On the other hand, acquiring pornography wasn't one of our collection development goals, either.

Why did I think *Sex* was pornographic? The book was filled with literally hundreds of photographs of Madonna in highly charged sexual tableaux. There was some text—maybe 10 pages out of 128—but I would say it was more incidental than intrinsic.

The reason the book generated so much free publicity is precisely because it wasn't the usual mass-market fare. Until then, books of similar format and content were found only in adult bookstores or through the mail. As indicated by the labeling and ID check, the publisher clearly intended the book for an adult audience.

The religious right often accuses public libraries of ignoring community standards. But do we?

Public libraries only buy materials that have been released by the community of publishers. We only know about materials advertised by the community of advertisers and reviewers.

And does it strike anyone else as odd that you don't find a big collection of X-rated videos or skin magazines at even big public libraries? Are we to take this as just an amazing coincidence?

Or do we take it for what it is—evidence that we do have collection standards and those standards are derived from our culture? We do know—just as Madonna does—how far we can walk along the edge of the cultural norm.

In America, the edge is somewhere in the vicinity of pictures of naked ladies, especially naked ladies engaged in sexual sport. I'm not saying this makes a whole lot of sense. I'm saying that in the main, librarians respect it.

Now it happens that our library did buy Bret Ellis's *American Psycho*—a book that seriously offended me, and whose content is grotesquely pornographic. So why didn't I buy *Sex?*

The difference is the preponderance of photographs. *Sex* had them. *American Psycho* didn't.

As I read the cultural consensus, most Americans seem to feel that if a book consists mostly of words on the page, then whatever pictures it summons in your own mind are your own business. But if the pictures are on the page, then the content somehow becomes more visceral.

While a parent might be upset that a child had access to *American Psycho*, the child at least has to read it to understand it. Literacy is its own defense. But this same child could glance at one of the more dubious photos in *Sex*—say the scene where Madonna is being raped in the gymnasium—and something would get communicated. The image has more immediacy.

At about this time, I realized that libraries don't set cultural standards. We reflect them, in all their complexity and contradictions. These standards don't change just because Madonna says they do. On the other hand, she may well have been a leading indicator.

Madonna's truly brilliant marketing and consequent financial success may well encourage others to publish similar books. On the day that such books become mainstream—available from your local grocery store and no longer exciting impassioned commentary—they will also appear in libraries.

Is There Life after Sex?

My decision not to buy the book was highlighted on the front page of the October 23, 1993, *Denver Post*—as I discovered, to my extreme discomfort, while standing in my driveway at 6:30 A.M. in my pajamas. But I couldn't help noticing that the *Post* had put all librarians in a puzzling position: Whether you bought the book or not, suddenly you found yourself working for Madonna.

That's worth a moment's reflection, too. Why would a newspaper, presumably an ally in literacy and opposition to censorship, do so much to create a controversy, then swing around and aim it at libraries?

Answer: The greater value to the newspaper is the selling of advertising. If people are reading about a scandal, they are also flipping past the ads.

This was also an object lesson in the power of the press. Even after an interview, what gets represented to the public is not necessarily what you thought was important. It's what the reporter and editor chose from your words, and how they chose to frame them. This underscored for me the great value of having your own newspaper column, where you can edit your words carefully and do your own framing.

So the next week, I walked through the reasoning behind my decision in the weekly column I write for the *Douglas County News Press*. I told people that although I didn't buy that book, we didn't buy a lot of books. *Sex* would still be available through interlibrary loan.

I also asked our patrons to let me know if they thought I had overstepped my boundaries and imposed censorship on them. A collection decision doesn't get any more public than that.

Now here's a curious thing. I got more mail and phone calls about my Madonna decision than I had received in my previous twenty years as a public librarian. In fact, for a time, I became something of a statewide clearinghouse for Madonna-related information. (My favorite clipping came from an Erma Bombeck column, wherein she wrote, "Will somebody please notice this girl?") With only two exceptions, all of the comments I received from the public were positive, even grateful.

The comments I got from librarians tended to be somewhat less supportive, ranging from the outraged to the irritated to the distinctly amused. I also spoke to a few librarians who believed I had made an absolutely unprofessional, indefensible, and wholly contemptible decision. Curiously, none of them purchased the book, either.

I mentioned earlier that our library had received more than its share of materials challenges. For a while after my Madonna decision, that slowed down. I took some comfort in the fact that while I may have astonished my friends, I completely confounded my critics.

I also wrote in an article I did for *Colorado Libraries*, "You have to hand it to Madonna. She made yet another fortune simply by making lots of people all across the country, if only for a few weeks, feel 'like a virgin.' Properly viewed, it's kind of sweet."

Focus on the Family

First Challenges

By the early 1990s, I was the new director of a county library system. In the process of making the rounds of my neighbors, I met with the local school media services coordinator. "How are things?" I asked.

She made polite small talk for a while, then said something unexpected: "I think I might be in trouble."

The school district had received a challenge in an elementary school regarding the book *Halloween ABC's*. Soon the schools would be going back to the voters for a bond issue. Administrative staff had made it very clear that they did not want controversy. It wasn't clear if that also meant appeasement.

The media services coordinator was resolved to live up to professional standards. She had followed all the steps; the complaint had been reviewed by a committee; considerable research had been done about its connection to and support of district curricular goals. Finally, the review committee had made its recommendation to retain the title.

But the librarian was still worried. I thought she was right to be.

So I made a call to the school superintendent, whom I'd had lunch with some weeks previous. "I just wanted to let you know that the Colorado library community has heard about this book challenge, and is very worried. We've noticed a disturbing trend in our schools. Someone raises a complaint. The book may or may not be removed. But shortly after that, the school board itself is taken over by people who believe their mission is to censor. I wanted to let you know that I'll be at this meeting, with several other concerned librarians."

He thanked me. Successful superintendents are savvy politicians, and they appreciate advance notice of regional social and political factors.

The woman who filed the complaint sat in the front row of the packed room and listened attentively to the report of the reconsideration committee. The committee recommended that the book be retained, but "monitored for age appropriateness."

That didn't sound good to me. How would that be decided, exactly? I know children who are wise beyond their years and adults who may never attain true maturity of judgment. What if a first-grader happened to slip it past the librarian? What might happen to the librarian if somebody complained? That didn't seem to bother anyone else.

The school superintendent found my eyes in the audience. He said in a clear, ringing tone that although in his judgment, the book wasn't especially good, censorship was an overriding issue in the case: His final decision was to accept the committee's recommendation and retain the book.

Then the woman who filed the complaint asked to address the board. And for perhaps forty-five minutes, she gave a highly detailed, poised, professional, point-by-point refutation of the committee's comments. Finally, she asked that the board overturn the superintendent's decision and remove the book.

During and after her comments, the audience was silent.

Then I spoke to the board. My comments took less than a minute. I said that there was an emerging pattern in Colorado: There were mounting numbers of attacks on the library collections of elementary schools, generally on materials believed to be offensive to the religious right. I said that in many cases, school board positions were taken over by people intent on removing library materials. "Our county is growing very rapidly," I said. "Surely, we need more books in our libraries, not fewer." To my genuine surprise, I got a big round of applause, sustained for at least a minute.

I've thought about it since then, and now I have two explanations for that. First, it pays to be brief. After the onslaught of the previous speaker, I believe I would have gotten applause for anything under five minutes.

Second, the teachers and parents in the crowd didn't like the twin prospects of ideological bullying and public appeasement. This was their first opportunity to express that.

The board voted to uphold the superintendent's decision. But the margin was narrow: four to three.

By the following Monday, I had received four written challenges to books held by our public library.

Vanity of the Bonfires

My staff got an interesting series of phone calls. One caller, who refused to be identified and refused to talk to me directly, set the pattern for the rest. She had three questions: Is the director a volunteer position? (No.) Who hires him? (The board of trustees.) How do you get on the board? (Library trustees are appointed by the county commissioners.)

There's more than one way to respond to this kind of situation. One is to be quiet and hope it all blows over. I believe this is the road most often taken.

Another is the opposite: to seek circuses and spotlights. I recommend it. If you hunker down and hide behind the Freedom to Read statement, you may earn the admiration of your peers, but you don't change any minds in your community. Better, I thought, to take the show on the road, find out who was behind all this, how many of them there were, and what they were really after.

So I announced a series of talks to be held at four of my library district's branches. I called the series, "Sense and Censorship: The Vanity of the Bonfires," which I swiped from a 1992 brochure by Marcia Pally, published by the Freedom to Read Foundation.

At these talks, I highlighted the kinds of complaints I had received and how the library responded. I handed out a list of banned books, with the reasons for the complaints underneath—always a crowd-pleaser.

I talked about the role of the public library as a gathering place for many different points of view. I talked about how important it was for parents to pay attention to what their kids read and to talk to them about those books.

While attendance varied at the meetings from as many as forty to as few as three, I did identify a core group of people who described themselves as "concerned" about the library. These people were very articulate and well prepared and had a couple of zingers.

"Why is it," one person asked, "that when a parent asks that an inappropriate book be removed from the library, we're immediately labeled 'censors'? Parents can't censor the library. Only the government can censor." He was right.

Another zinger followed: "Do you approve of the classics?" I walked right into it. What librarian doesn't? Reading the classics, I said, improved the mind, deepened your understanding of humanity, provided a rich appreciation for the drama of nature.

"Then you would agree," said one woman, "that if good books make you better, bad books make you worse!"

Gotcha.

Because, of course, I was wrong. Good books don't make you better, not all by themselves, anymore than looking at an apple makes you healthier. A book has to be selected and digested. Its content must not just be read, but chosen.

In fact, much of what we read or view has little effect on us at all. Reading requires conscious effort. Adding something to your belief system doesn't happen automatically.

The Literature of the Right

Consulting a magazine in her lap, one woman asked, "Why doesn't the library have any of these books?" It was a list of what I think can be accurately described as conservative Christian titles. Among them were *Aborted Women—Silent No More; Men and Marriage; Idols for Destruction: Christian Faith and Its Confrontation with American Society; Weak Link: The Feminization of the American Military;* and *Society of the West.* I'd never heard of any of them. The woman continued, "Isn't the library, in fact, censoring these materials by deliberately not purchasing them?"

First, I said that not choosing to buy a book doesn't constitute censorship. When you buy a Honda, it doesn't mean that you're deliberating boycotting Toyota. Similarly, there are lots of books the library doesn't buy that we don't necessarily oppose.

Commercial presses publish more than a hundred and fifty thousand titles each year. We can't possibly buy all of them, and probably wouldn't if we could.

Second, I said the library was more than willing to track down books that people wanted to read. It is the policy at our library to purchase almost anything a patron asks for, the exceptions being those titles that are prohibitively expensive or on some highly obscure or technical subject.

Then I asked if I could borrow the magazine she was reading from, so that I could get enough information about the titles to try to track them down. I also asked for her name and phone number, so I could call her when they came in.

I repeated that offer a lot, and I compiled quite a list of materials.

I quickly learned that most of the titles people requested had been featured in *Citizen*, a publication of FOF, an evangelical Christian organization operating out of Colorado Springs and founded and then headed by Dr. James Dobson.

I went to the head of our technical services department and said, "I want to buy every one of these. It's important that we track them down and get them on the shelves as rapidly as possible. I need to demonstrate that the library is serious about responding to its patrons—all of them." She had the whole list on the shelf within a week.

Then I wrote a letter to the people who had attended the workshops. "These are new materials acquired by the library. Thank you for your suggestions. Note, too, the existence of many similar titles already owned by the library. This is your library, too, and we do want you to find materials that represent your perspective. As with all of our purchases, we will be watching to determine the use of these collections."

Many of these people later contacted me. Originally suspicious, they were surprised, then pleased, then thoughtful.

FOF had told them that Christians of their political persuasion deserved a place at the table of public discourse. This is the lament of many minorities, and Christian evangelicals are but one.

In the following months, I debated two of FOF's key policy analysts at different library events. I said to one of them, "Welcome to the table! But your seat doesn't entitle you to demand that everyone else leave or remain silent. The library will listen to your concerns. Will you listen to the concerns of others?"

At the end of each debate, I extended an invitation. "Thank you for coming to our meeting. I hope you were treated respectfully." The answer was always yes. "Good," I would say, "and in return, I would like to offer my time to come to one of your gatherings." The answer was always, "We've never done that." To my knowledge, FOF still hasn't.

I believe this is a matter of importance. Colorado librarians went out of their way to invite our most outspoken critics into our internal debates. Our critics continued to shut us out of their policy discussions.

Some years later, our library came under attack from another group of conservative Christians. But I learned through the grapevine that this earlier group of library users intervened. "We like the library," they said. "It provides extraordinary support for our homeschool efforts. And here's a list of books and videos the library purchased at our request. The library," they said, "is our friend."

Oh, and the books the library purchased from FOF circulated very well.

Reading with the Enemy

I didn't just buy this stuff. I started reading it, too. It was fascinating. Take *Citizen*. The title of one article was "Books You Won't Find in a Public Library." Author Brian Mitchell wrote, "Many libraries do not stock books that criticize feminism, abortion, or homosexuality. So much for 'free speech.'" The article also contained the statement, "Library workers are 'very liberal, very leftist,' says an employee of the New York Public Library."

My reaction to this was mixed. On the one hand, it amused me to see the way librarians were presented. ("Hey, Vito, one of the boys at NYPL has been talkin', see? They're on to us. Lean on 'im. I want things quiet, real quiet.")

On the other hand, if these books really were seen by conservatives as "significant contributions to the literature available on important current issues," then why didn't libraries have them? Granted, the occasionally bitter, inflammatory tone of the author could be explained by the fact that his own book (*Weak Link*, above) didn't do well in the library market, and maybe that was because it wasn't a very good book. But just because someone is cranky doesn't mean he's wrong.

As noted above, I discovered that the conservative challenges to my library's collection, almost without exception, came from people who subscribed to *Citizen*. And a lot of the arguments these people used were lifted right out of *Citizen*'s pages.

It seemed to me that it would be useful to hear those arguments ahead of time, so I could better respond. There was only one thing to do: I joined FOF. And then, because a lot of FOF stuff was about People For the American Way (Norman Lear's anticensorship watchdog group, also known as People For), I joined them, too.

My mail began to get really interesting.

For one thing, I always seemed to get their publications on the same day. I would read them back-to-back.

For another, FOF and People For mostly talked about each other. Neither one of them had much good to say. FOF, according to People For, were trying to impose a theocracy on the American public. People For, according to FOF, were urging abortion and advancing the radical gay agenda.

But there was another difference. When not railing at their enemies, FOF publications were warm and folksy. They had color photographs of cute families. They had parenting tips and columns with an avuncular or ministerial bent. The world was presented as fraught with danger, but that's why FOF existed: to provide encouragement, support, and counseling.

By contrast, People For publications were written by lawyers for lawyers. There was a battle going on in that world, too, but it was fought by people in suits. The language was cerebral and shrill, not warmly emotional. There were no heartfelt stories about women who had to tend sick or "willful" children when money was tight and the husband was gone. There were no lush pictures of families gathered together on a picnic.

It was perfectly obvious who was going to win.

Incidentally, People For the American Way, founded by Norman Lear, was originally intended to do just what FOF was doing—provide a media-savvy advocacy for a point of view. In my judgment, it has drifted far from that position. In the process, it has become less effective.

Community Impact Seminar

In November 1992, I signed up for a Community Impact Seminar sponsored by two groups: FOF and an associated group called the Rocky Mountain Family Council, formed by a group of conservative lawyers.

Both groups have described themselves as conservative Christian. Each sought to be far more visible in what FOF likes to call "the public square"—the world of politics and public affairs.

The day-long workshop was held at a mega-church in Colorado Springs. The house was packed. The speakers tended to be lively, funny, and very comfortable on stage.

I attended with a reporter for the *Denver Post* who had recently written about the interlocking directorships of a number of evangelical and political groups. Clearly, she concluded, there was a core group of people working for some specific ends.

When we signed in together, we were asked to specify our church membership. My friend was a Quaker. I was, and am, "unchurched."

The first point, communicated humorously, was about the need for people of faith to come together, to set aside doctrinal differences to work on those beliefs they held in common.

There was plenty of opportunity for public questions. One person asked about abortion, to which the speaker replied that many Christian leaders believed this was the defining moral issue of our times, as crucial as slavery had been before the Civil War. (I did not offer that it took many years before the Southern Baptists apologized for their pre–Civil War approval of slavery.)

Shortly after that, the lone African American woman in the crowd stood up. She said she was disappointed to see so few people of color in the audience. The speaker said he shared that disappointment and that the evangelical movement needed to do a better job.

The seminar proceeded until one of the speakers was handed a note from the registration desk and a copy of my friend's *Denver Post* article. The speaker then switched to a fairly savage denunciation of the article and the author. My friend and I looked at each other. "This is interesting!" she said.

Later in the seminar Tom Minnery spoke, then representing the Rocky Mountain Family Council. He talked about two cases involving public schools in Aurora, Colorado.

In the first case, some parents who were upset about the possibility of school-sponsored distribution of condoms to high school students contacted the Rocky Mountain Family Council for help. The council responded with a barrage of medical evidence and legal opinions about the use and distribution of condoms.

After considering this information, the school's health task force— and eventually the whole school board—changed their minds. The plan to distribute condoms was dropped, and according to the speaker, the board was going to develop a new sex education program based on abstinence.

If all this indeed happened as described, I would characterize it as "the politics of consensus." Some local people sought relevant information from at least one outside source and presented it to local decision makers. Everybody talked about it. The final decision was therefore better informed.

I think that's good. I even think it's commendable, although I am not an advocate of abstinence-only education.

Then Minnery talked about a more disturbing case. An elementary school student checked out a book called *Witches* from the school library. His parents were upset, partly by the subject matter, and partly by some of the drawings in the book. Again, a call was made to the Rocky Mountain Family Council.

This time, the council used press releases to prod local Denver TV channel 7 into interviewing the parents. On that night's news, the station showed some pictures from the book—but with little black strips across the alleged "naughty bits."

According to the seminar spokesperson, the unnamed school principal then acted quickly and covertly. First, he told the school librarian to remove *Witches* from the collection. Then he ordered her to yank any and all books with words like "witch," or "ghost," or "Halloween" in the title. Permanently.

At this point in the seminar more than six hundred people burst into sustained and impassioned applause.

Now this story, if true, bothered me a lot. This is not the politics of consensus. It is the politics of intimidation and appeasement. This is not the reasoned consideration of objective data. It is the blind rejection of a whole branch of literature solely to avoid the pall of "bad PR."

Folk and fairy tales—many of which feature witches—are a long-standing part of our mainstream cultural heritage. To remove a list of unexamined materials solely on the basis of the words in their titles is blatant censorship—official government action to ban materials.

But the intent of the group was clear. The speakers urged the congregation/seminar attendees to target school board elections, library board appointments, the Republican Party leadership, and a broad range of elected positions. Then they described some fairly practical ways to put evangelical Christians in charge of the apparatus of government.

Much of the political advice was lifted right out of the sixties. Come up with names for a local organization that sounded grassroots, that did not tip off the media to a religious connection. For example, use words like "taxpayer," or "concerned citizens for" instead of "Christians for."

Party politics in Colorado use a caucus system, a sort of precinct presbytery. Instructions were given for how to track announcements of upcoming caucuses, how many people were necessary to show up, how to go about becoming a representative to the larger caucus, and how to get a resolution or nomination passed.

Let me make this clear: This careful coaching on how government works is good civics.

In a democracy, any group has the right to champion its beliefs, to try to persuade others to change their beliefs, and to seek to influence public policy.

Any group that takes the time to get organized, to inform itself about the political process, or even to assume the often thankless jobs of public service in the first place, can have a great effect on our culture.

When public agencies are strapped for funds, such political activists may wield even greater influence. School districts, libraries, and elected officials may shy away from any controversy lest they face voter defeat on entirely unrelated issues.

And in official silence, through back-door appeasements and capitulation, a single group can impose its values on an entire public institution.

My friend and I came away from the meeting thoughtful and subdued. A few weeks later, I noticed an announcement in our local newspaper. There was a new group in town. They called themselves the Concerned Douglas County Taxpayers (CDCT).

Concerned Douglas County Taxpayers

The first meeting of this new group was scheduled at the library, one of the few free, publicly available meeting places that was not tied to a church. The announcement in the paper was precisely the kind of clear-but-coded statement the Community Impact Seminar had prescribed: This group of "taxpayers" had "concerns" about the need for abstinence-based sex education in the schools. They had concerns about outcome-based education, a new movement among public schools. They had concerns about books in the library, although they didn't say whether they meant school or public or both.

By this time, I had written a number of newspaper columns about the library's stand for intellectual freedom. I decided to attend the meeting.

There were about eighty people. When I walked in, eighty heads swiveled as one and glared at me as if I were the devil himself. (My picture was featured above my newspaper column.) It was an uncomfortable feeling.

The speaker, a local man, got up and talked about how he hoped this new organization would have a positive effect on the community. He brought up, and thanked, a representative from the Rocky Mountain Family Council for assistance in getting organized. The connection to FOF was not stated.

Then the speaker went through an agenda, a list of concerns.

"We need to do something about sex education in the schools!" Judging by the nodding of heads, there was considerable agreement.

He went down the list until he got to "books in the library." Again, every head turned to me. I smiled.

"And you can read the rest," he said.

"Not for long," I thought.

But then the group broke up into smaller groups to work on developing some positions about the topics.

I floated among the groups to hear their concerns. One group grappled with possibilities for collecting impact fees from developers to offset the costs of new neighborhoods. One woman looked thoughtful. "Hmm," she said. "We're all Christians, yet we can't agree!"

And my attitude began to change. First, it was good that the people who were concerned about the library, came to the library to talk. Second, it was good that the talk was frank. They admitted they were Christians, but were discovering that this orientation didn't automatically sort out a host of complex issues.

Another group was very suspicious of outcome-based education, which they believed was a liberal plan to teach critical thinking at the cost of curricular content.

I was something of an educational activist myself in those days. My wife and I were homeschooling our daughter, and I was an outspoken critic of the school system's inability to clearly articulate just what a child was supposed to know at the end of a school year. I had been active in forming one of Colorado's first charter schools.

I settled into that group, and we talked.

At the end of the meeting, a collection was taken up for newsletter costs. I handed over my $5 and got a wry grin from the taker.

At the next meeting, I had set up a display of materials about outcome-based education, both for and against. I also had a copy or two of articles about developer fees.

This time, I was greeted by name. I could see people pawing through the materials. They told me the names of other authors. I promised to get them.

By the end of that meeting, some of us were comparing notes on our kids.

Several weeks later, I was at a meeting at the school board. The leader of the CDCT walked into the room, and the eighty teachers in attendance swung their heads to him and glared as if *he* were the devil himself.

A week or so after that, the leader came to my office. "Some of our members are concerned about your attendance at our meetings," he said. "They think you have an agenda. I told them, well, let's just ask him. He'll tell us."

"Thanks for coming in," I said. "I will be honest with you. I share many of your concerns, especially about the need for clear curriculum. I'll support you on that. In other areas, I don't know if I support you or not. I'm still listening and learning. But I am absolutely opposed to your attempts to get books out of libraries, and I'll stand up and say so. I don't think you understand just what libraries are supposed to do."

We talked for a while, and I told him about the many books we'd bought by FOF. I talked about how we had done a survey earlier that year asking people if they felt we should be more careful about books in the library, and got a ringing endorsement from them (about sixteen to one) against censorship of any kind.

But I emphasized this point: "It's perfectly reasonable to expect that you will find materials that are sympathetic to your views here. You are a taxpayer, and I take the obligation to be a good steward of your contribution very seriously. But it is not reasonable to forbid other people, also taxpayers, from finding materials that support their views."

I said, "I'll defend those other books from your attacks. But I'll also defend yours from theirs, with just as much passion."

When he left, we were able to shake hands.

Here's what I learned from all this: It is too easy to demonize our enemies. But it's easiest when you don't actually have to talk to them. Showing up at their meetings, providing information on topics of interest to them, listening to their concerns before I articulated mine was a strategy that led not to victory but to something rarer and more precious: mutual respect.

The Church of Jesus Christ of Latter-Day Saints

My third lesson came through an encounter with another religious group, the Mormons, or more properly, the Church of Jesus Christ of Latter-Day Saints (LDS).

My first conscious encounter with them was when we expanded a storefront library to grab hold of the next bay. A woman with a wonderful smile, let's call her Donna, showed up to offer volunteers. She had Boy Scouts looking for community projects. She also had some people from her church who were willing to help.

She and her troops showed up to move books, dust shelves, drag carts around, and generally provide a lot of much needed and appreciated grunt work.

Sometime later, Donna came back with a request that the library purchase a reference work about the church. We did.

Then I got a letter from the president of the Church Stake, the regional unit of the LDS. It was accompanied by a letter from the Anti-Defamation League. The president was Donna's husband. She hand-delivered the letter.

In brief, the letter protested a video owned by the very same library she had helped set up. The title was *The God Makers*. In fact, there was another one, a follow-up called *The God Makers II*.

The letter made various allegations: The video was incendiary; it was false; it was libelous; it was, because of its documentary-style approach, credible to the uninformed. It was, in fact, an inflammatory example of religious bigotry. Finally, the letter requested that we remove the items immediately.

I asked our manager how we'd come by the title. She said the first video had been a patron request, and a quick review of various sources hadn't revealed much. Since we acquired it, though, it had circulated very well. So when the request for the second title came in, we bought that, too.

At the time, I had two ministers in my neighborhood. One was pastor of an evangelical Lutheran denomination. I asked him if he'd heard of the video. He had. Although he hadn't seen it himself, he heard that some of the more fundamentalist churches showed it as a caution against "false religions."

Down the street lived another minister, the head of a fundamentalist Baptist church. Had he heard of it? "Oh yes," he said, "I've shown it at my church many times." He hadn't gotten it from the library.

I searched other library catalogs and found that we were virtually the only owner of the title in the state.

When the video came back in, I watched it. Then I sent the following letter.

Library Letter to the Church

September 12, 1994

Dear Donna:

Thank you for your heartfelt interest in our library. As always, you are an articulate and effective spokesperson of the LDS. I do take your concerns very seriously.

Thank you, too, for your attachments (the letter from your Stake president, the Anti-Defamation League release, and the statement from the National Conference of Christians and Jews). In accordance with our policies, I'm attaching some things for you, too. These are the guiding visions of my profession and the standards we try, sometimes with difficulty, to live up to. I've also attached a copy of our complaint policy—the steps we follow when someone fills out a "citizen's request for reconsideration of library materials form," as you have done.

I wanted to clarify some of the circumstances surrounding our purchase of *The God Makers I* and *II*. We did not seek it out; a Highlands Ranch Library patron requested it, just as you requested that the library purchase Daniel H. Ludlow's five-volume *Encyclopedia of Mormonism*. In both cases, we complied (although we probably spent more time researching your request because of the relatively high cost of the encyclopedia). We have just one copy of each videotape; there are no others in the library district.

Since the time it was added, *The God Makers I* has gone out forty-two times. *The God Makers II* has gone out thirty-two times. That's fairly brisk business for a videotape that isn't either a feature film or a how-to. On the whole, that's discouraging news; this videotape has an audience. (Although there's no way to know how many different individuals checked it out—it could have been one person checking it out many times.)

Again, in accordance with our policies, I have reviewed both tapes in their entirety. In many respects, I agree with you, with your Stake president, and with the Anti-Defamation League. The tapes do indeed "draw upon the incendiary arsenal of religious bigotry," as Gillian Martin Soren-sen writes.

But I disagree that the appropriate response to this is to "pull those videotapes off our shelves" or "to eliminate false information and defaming accusations" by "removing *The God Makers I* and *II* . . . and all such mate-rials from any other libraries . . ."

That may seem contradictory to you. Doesn't the library want to have materials that contain factual, unbiased information—information that will help establish a climate of understanding and tolerance? We do.

But it is a painful truth of our time that such works are in short supply. On almost any political or religious issue, far too many works distort the truth, malign (on scant evidence) the people they believe to be their oppo-nents, and seek to foster hate.

Your Stake president writes that "no one should ridicule sacred things." Perhaps not. But if libraries applied that principle to book selection, we'd be hard-pressed to buy much of anything. Virtually every work of modern fiction is sprinkled with profanity, especially those titles on the best-seller list. Many popular works of non-fiction are distinctly polarized—liberals call conservatives fascists and Nazis; conservatives call liberals baby-killers and perverts.

Buying materials from any particular religious perspective presents its own problems. We have books by fundamentalists that mock centuries of bib-lical scholarship, and books of biblical scholarship that directly challenge the most fervent beliefs of fundamentalists (for instance, "inerrancy"). The library has a copy of Thomas Paine's *Age of Reason*, challenged throughout two centuries as blasphemous. We have a copy of Hitler's *Mein Kampf*, a book of virulent anti-Semitism. All of these ridicule some things people hold sacred.

One solution might be to avoid the subject of religion all together, as our public schools have done. But surely we should expect more from a public library than silence.

Another solution might be to collect nothing but academic "surveys" of religion, providing innocuous histories and neutral primers. In this way libraries would neither offend—nor satisfy—anyone.

A third and, I believe, better solution is to try to identify some of the representative texts of many perspectives, in the belief that our patrons are smart enough to look at the historical and current cultural evidence and sort it all out for themselves. We librarians have neither the wisdom nor the authority to make such decisions for them.

As I told you on the phone, *The God Makers I* and *II* don't discredit the Mormon Church. If anything, in my opinion they reveal just how bigoted, hys-terical, and pitifully stupid anti-Mormonism can be. I suspect that the only people likely to watch such videotapes all the way through are people who have already made up their minds about the subject. The Anti-Defamation League states that *The God Makers II* "utilizes a documentary-like style with a factual tone to project a high degree of believability." I find that statement astonishing. I found *The God Makers II* unbelievable to the point of absurdity.

Your Stake president said three more things that deserve further comment.

First, when he writes that "members of our community should not par-ticipate in the religious bigotry and hatred that are so common throughout the world," I infer that he believes making *The God Makers* available for public viewing constitutes "participation." Rather, I believe that in order to defend yourself against bigotry, you have to be able to track it. You have to seek out the evidence and drag it into the light. The best way to deal with this kind of sensationalist hate-mongering is exposure, not suppression.

Second, your Stake president writes that "We have confidence and respect in people of faith. We feel certain that once they have determined what is true, they will have no part in promoting this videotape." The library owns many materials. We don't "promote" any of them. We just present them, making it possible for people to "determine what is true" based on their own examination, not the library's predetermined conclusions.

Third, he states that "the videotape contains charges of immorality and misuse of church funds by church leaders. These charges are blatantly false." If he's right, and it wouldn't surprise me, then why don't those leaders sue the makers of the video for libel? Defamation of character is most properly a finding of the courts, not the public library.

It is an article of faith within my profession that good information drives out the bad. Accordingly, I believe that the Douglas County Libraries needs to buy some videotapes that are more sympathetic to Mormon beliefs, to be shelved right beside *The God Makers*. In reviewing our circulation collection, it appears to me we have more negative portrayals of Mormonism than positive, an accident of mainstream publishing choices and public requests. We should do something about that. I can't guarantee we'll buy everything you recommend, but I will make a good-faith effort to acquire a representative sample and seek better balance in the library collection.

I am hereby soliciting from you a list of videotapes you believe provide either a direct counter to *The God Makers I* and *II* (if such a tape exists), and/or a more positive introduction to the tenets of your faith. I'm sure many people are simply curious about LDS. *The God Makers I* and *II* aren't much of an introduction, except to demonstrate that Mormons are one of many targets of religious intolerance.

Too, we will also buy *The Truth about the God Makers*. I'll give you a call if I have trouble tracking it down.

Finally, then, I have decided to retain the videotapes.

If you wish to protest this decision, you do have the option of appealing it to my bosses, the board of trustees. Their decision is final. If you'd like to pursue this option, give me a call, and I'll schedule you at the top of our next meeting, which is at 7 P.M., September 24, 1994, at the Oakes Mill Library in the Lone Tree subdivision. The board meets monthly; if you can't make this one, just let me know what would be more convenient.

I also intend, unless you have some objection, to raise this issue in one of my newspaper columns. It's the classic dilemma of the public library: What is the right response to bigotry? How can the library make a positive contribution to our culture without assuming the role of censor?

Thank you again for your concern. I hope this response—although it isn't what you asked for—does at least shed some light on our aims and our challenges.

Church Response to the Letter

A week or so went by after I sent the letter. Then I got a phone call from Donna. She was friendly but cautious. "Let me understand this," she said. "You're not going to pull the video."

"Right," I said.

"But you are willing to add more materials, positive materials, about our church."

"Yes," I said.

We talked further, and she said she wasn't sure if the church could provide them for free. I said that was fine; I was prepared to buy the materials from our library budget. My budget wasn't unlimited, of course, but I would indeed make a good-faith effort (no pun intended) to balance our collection on this subject. She wanted to know how much I was willing to spend. I told her I didn't know. But if she could provide a list of recommended titles and costs, I would do the best I could.

Another week or so went by, and I got a list of materials in the mail. It was a reasonably thorough review of the historic development of the LDS and a collection of some key writings on various topics from the Mormon perspective. It was an honest response to my request, and thoughtfully grouped by suggested purchase and cost. If I bought the first group, it would set back the library about $300.

My staff checked out the entire list, and the titles were all from reputable sources, several outside the church. To purchase every title on the bibliography would cost about $2,000.

So we bought all of it. Here's why.

Back then, there were about fifty thousand Mormons in the south Denver area. Today, eleven years later, there are closer to two hundred thousand. There was a constituency for the topic and a strong probability that the titles would be used. (They have been.)

Our library had done a demonstrably poor job of representing the perspective of this growing group. It was a collection development project that was timely.

The group that approached us with its concern had treated us decently: helping us with various projects ahead of time, providing a formal declaration of their concerns, responding positively and quickly to our proposed solution.

We were a rapidly growing library, with the money to respond to the request.

As with the CDCT, we managed to show we were serious both about our stand for intellectual freedom and our commitment to representing the perspectives of our patrons.

There were a couple of follow-ups to this episode. First, I was invited by Donna to meet at a young LDS couple's house, not far from us. It turned out that they had a son, born at home, delivered by the same midwives who had delivered ours. I had a lovely evening at their place, talking with them, Donna and her husband, and observing firsthand the strong social ties and solid family life of most LDS members.

I told Donna afterward that I had enjoyed the evening very much, but that I was not interested in becoming a member of her church. She was worried that she had somehow offended me or misrepresented the church. I assured her that she had not. Rather, I suspected that I would be a poor fit for her church, or any other, chafing as I do under anything that resembles adult supervision. She laughed.

Some years later, I was the president of what was the Colorado Library Association (now known as the Colorado Association of Libraries after a merger with the school library association). Donna approached me again with some friends. The LDS had put together an outreach program for public libraries in the state. It included a collection of some of those core materials, paid for by local churches, and ready to be mailed to libraries.

I strongly approved of the project and wrote a cover letter endorsing it. I made it clear that I was not a Mormon and that no public or association money had been used in the effort. But I underscored two facts: the growth of the church in Colorado and the state of bias of my own collection before I took a closer look at it. I urged receiving librarians to review the materials, and if they found them as solid as I had, to add them to their collections.

I heard from one or two librarians who received the package. I believe most of them were indeed added to their catalogs.

I have maintained very positive relations with LDS members and have worked with them in a variety of settings.

The Difference between FOF and the Mormons

There are several significant differences between FOF and LDS.

FOF has, following the layoff or reassignment of some seventy-nine employees in September 2005, more than twelve hundred employees and an annual budget of about $143 million. It has, according to Right Wing Watch, 2.3 million subscribers to its ten monthly magazines. Moreover, its primary spokesperson, Dr. Dobson, reaches an estimated two hundred million people every day through the radio. FOF is not a church, but its members are largely Protestant fundamentalists.

LDS has more than twelve million members worldwide and more than five million in the United States. According to a *Time Magazine* piece (August 4, 1997, p. 52), "Its current assets total a minimum of $30 billion. If it were a corporation, its estimated $5.9 billion in annual gross income would place it midway through the Fortune 500, a little below Union Carbide and the Paine Webber Group but bigger than Nike and the Gap."

Dobson is no longer the CEO of FOF. These days, he is mostly working on various political causes, mainly the appointment of Supreme Court justices who share his views.

Dobson's style very much sets the tone for FOF. Outside of his pediatric advice, he is frequently condemnatory in tone. When I joined FOF, I received his monthly letters. His themes are consistent: Christians are an oppressed majority in America, the victims of a liberal plot to separate religion from the state in violation of what he claims is the clear "Christian history" of the founding of the United States. Historically, he is utterly mistaken on every count, and perhaps deliberately misleading.

In general, Dobson's approach is to stir up his base, find a theme of fear and alarm, and conclude with an appeal for funds to fight this latest, or continuing, threat. The key enemies are liberals of any stripe, activist judges (who persist in interpreting the law on the basis of precedent and the Constitution), and homosexuals.

In 2003, I toured FOF with one of its public relations representatives. I believe FOF is in trouble. Its funds are not growing as they had been. The appeal of the message isn't playing as well with Gen-Xers as it did with the Boomers, for reasons described in the next chapter, entitled "Generations."

The Mormons, unlike the overwhelming Protestant majority in the United States, have frequently been, and continue to be, targeted for real religious discrimination, beginning with the assassination of their founder, Joseph Smith. This has made them cautious. They take a longer view, of steady, sustainable expansion. Their missions build political expertise and international connections. They assimilate slowly but thoroughly. They make allies in the community. They appeal to the young.

When comparing People For to FOF, I decided that FOF had the better tactics, the likeliest to succeed. Comparing FOF to the Mormons, I'd bet on the Mormons.

But aside from all that, it's clear that a significant number of library challenges have a religious base. The mother opposing *Big 16* was a fundamentalist. The challenge against Madonna's *Sex* was the work of a single conservative church. The CDCT was a religious group in grassroots costume. The Mormons are members of a highly organized religion.

It's worth looking a little deeper into why evangelical Christians—but not only evangelical Christians—challenge libraries.

Reading with the Enemy

The Premises of Censorship

I believe people do things for a reason, or several reasons. Those reasons may be false, confused, or inconsistent. But people's actions are not random.

I also believe that most people are good. By that I mean that people of widely different backgrounds can still agree about many essentials. We want ourselves and our children to be healthy. We want our cities to be safe, whether from local bullies and criminals or from international terrorists and armies. We want to be reasonably prosperous—free from poverty or privation. We want the freedom to pursue our interests and to be defended against the oppression by others. We want life, liberty, and the pursuit of happiness.

The list of premises below is an attempt to identify some of the recurrent themes adopted by the religious right, but again, not only by them.

The Book Made Me Do It

The first, and most crucial, is the belief in "the book made me do it." Behind the challenges of many patrons is awe of the written word. This may well be rooted in the profound respect granted to the Bible, based on several factors, but not least upon its endurance.

This belief, incidentally, is also shared by the secular left, which believes education—mainly, exposure to the written word—is also very powerful.

There is the belief that if you are a Christian and stumble across Tom Paine's *The Age of Reason,* you'll become an atheist (even though he was a deist). If you happen to be a feminist, but are for some reason forced to read a book by Cal Thomas, you will immediately renounce your sordid past and devote yourself gladly to the church, wifedom, and motherhood, in that order.

Dr. James Dobson, founder of FOF, was the man who interviewed serial killer Ted Bundy. Bundy, a notorious and pathological liar, said that he had become a killer because he'd gotten caught in the addictive cycle of pornography. Amazingly, Dobson bought it. Then he sold it—on his worldwide radio network and through his prolific writings.

Another familiar evangelical argument is that if books don't make you do things, then how can you explain the tremendous amount of time and money spent by those in the pornography, liquor, and cigarette industries to train and research the buying habits of the American buying public? Yet, absent such advertising, human beings, even those outside the United States, do seem to show persistent interest in both sex and consciousness-altering substances.

Behind the belief in the power of the word is the belief that humans are notoriously weak-willed, susceptible to temptation, and easily led astray. This belief, of course, is correct.

But perhaps "the book made me do it" is too harsh. Rephrase this to: Books matter. Who will not agree?

It's a Conspiracy

I mentioned that I got both FOF and People For publications in my mailbox. For all their cross-allegations, they had many areas of agreement. Here are three:

1. It's a conspiracy.
2. The other side is unscrupulous, underhanded, and cannot be trusted.
3. The other side is winning.

But let's talk about the conspiracy.

To some "the conspiracy" is the fundamentalist Christians against the secular humanists. The Supreme Court has consistently upheld freedom of expression, while clearly delineating the difference between religion and "secular humanism." Nonetheless, religion is gone from textbooks lest someone on one side or the other take offense at the bare facts of the past.

By way of an antidote, I came up with the notion that my library ought to sponsor a lecture series on world religions. I thought I could invite responsible spokespeople for both Christian and non-Christian denominations to come in and tell an audience what they stood for. For instance, I wasn't all that sure myself precisely what the difference was between a Presbyterian and a Methodist or why there were two synods of the Lutheran church. So I wrote a column about the lecture series idea for the local paper, hoping to gauge the public interest. The response was illustrative.

First, I got a call from a woman who told me that although she was a committed Christian, she thought the lecture series was a perfectly wonderful idea. Why? "Because those Mormons are up to something."

Next, I got a letter from a former union organizer with a long history of civil rights and anti-war activism. He wrote, "If you host this series, I'll sue the library. This is a direct violation of the separation of church and state."

Imagine. The First Amendment, which guarantees freedom of speech and freedom of religion at the same time, forbids us to talk about religion.

That was it. Nobody else expressed any desire for such a series at all. For a conspiracy, there sure is a lot of general agreement.

After all, just saying that you want something to happen doesn't mean that you've joined a conspiracy to make it so. This is America. There is no fundamentalist Christian or secular humanist conspiracy: There are just two groups of folks desperately trying to convince everyone else that the other side is crazy.

Why is this premise so popular? Because human beings are wired to respond to threats. It is often easier to motivate potential followers to avert a catastrophe than to accomplish some independent good.

Library Materials Should Reflect Community Standards

Another of the major premises of censorship is the notion that library materials should reflect community standards.

There are a number of responses, but the first one is simply, "When don't they?" We can only buy what the community of publishers chooses to print—and that, in turn, is determined by what the community of consumers is likely to buy.

This is by no means a defense of those choices. The continuing conglomeration of publishing houses, the American fascination with celebrity and fat, are not causes for celebration. But librarians can only buy what's on the market.

Beyond that, we only buy what we know about, which means we depend on the community of editors and reviewers to tell us what they think about the current stock.

Finally, any library worth its salt has some willingness to buy what its patrons ask for—or the library doesn't have supporters for long.

Add all those up, and it's hard to see how it's possible for us to reflect anything *but* the values of our various, interlocking communities. Libraries don't publish books, music, and films. We collect them.

Maybe that's too bad. Implicit in the notion of community standards is the idea that they are inherently correct.

How many libraries south of the Mason-Dixon Line in the 1950s had works by James Baldwin or Richard Wright? Of the libraries that did carry those works, how many of them reflected the standards of the community?

Sometimes it is precisely the books that most profoundly challenge the current standards that are most necessary.

Library Materials Should Present Only Positive Role Models

Another recurrent theme behind many recent challenges is the idea that library materials should only present positive role models.

One of the first complaints I ever received was about *Fade* by Robert Cormier. It was a story about a boy who could turn invisible—a powerful temptation for a teenager. A woman called me—she was very distressed that her child had found such filth in the public library. And then she read me how the young protagonist of the story, thirteen years old, lusted after his aunt.

How old was her child? Fourteen.

"Why," she asked me, "can't we have good, pure, clean, wholesome stories in our libraries?"

"Like the classics?" I asked.

"The classics!" she said with enthusiasm.

"I've got this one book I'm reading now," I said. "It's about two teenagers who have sex. They're not even fifteen. They eventually commit suicide."

"That's the kind of trash I'm talking about!" she said.

"*Romeo and Juliet*," I apologized.

Another woman called to tell me that she was upset that the library had a book called *Baby Love*—in which several high school girls had babies and dropped out of school. This book, the woman said, suggested that sex was pleasurable (*stop* the presses!) and that other girls would be encouraged to have babies, too.

But library materials tell stories. They present choices, not role models. In both *Fade* and *Baby Love*, the people lived, for want of a better phrase, "loose lives." And they were desperately unhappy and suffered for it. Maybe the people who read about such life choices won't be doomed to repeat them. They'll have a little better idea of the consequences. Literature is vicarious living.

Remember: There is no safer sex than just reading about it.

A corollary of the positive role model idea is that, somehow, fiction should never be unpleasant. We had one complaint about the *Little Red Riding Hood* version where, at the end, Red is floating, whole, in the wolf's belly. Outside falls the shadow of the woodsman, ax in hand.

"This could be disturbing to small children," read the complaint.

I would hope so, I wanted to respond. People forget that in the original version of *Little Red Riding Hood*, Granny and Red were goners. There was no woodsman.

There was, however, a lesson: Don't talk to strangers.

There's a popular misconception that fairy tales are innocent—frothy tales of sheer, whimsical fun. Some years ago now, the editor of *Chinaberry* (a distributor for children's material) recounted in her catalog, somewhat uneasily, how her own daughter showed a distinct preference for the darker, original fairy tales of the Brothers Grimm. The mother preferred the ones that had been cleaned up, made less sexist or violent. But often, especially when she was reading the really grim ones, her daughter's eyes glittered with excitement; she would ask them to be read to her again and again.

The late Bruno Bettelheim, in his *The Uses of Enchantment: The Meaning and Importance of Fairy Tales*, told us why. The purpose of many fairy tales was to prepare us to deal with the many crushing blows of life: the loss or cruelty of a parent, the horrors of war, the specter of starvation. By hearing these stories, by working through the patterns of crisis and resolution, children, in a deep place in their minds, developed some coping strategies. The stories they ask for are the stories that waken and name their own real fears. Parents do not do their children a service to protect them too fiercely, lest they never form imaginative antibodies to the many intellectual and emotional illnesses of existence.

And back to *Romeo and Juliet:* At the core of every classic is conflict. Conflict isn't always pleasant.

Humor Has No Place in Libraries

Most of all, I find that people somehow forget that everything doesn't have to be serious.

I got one complaint about *The Stupids Die*. A parent told me that no children should be called "stupid." Why? Because it might be damaging to their self-esteem.

I responded as I often did when I received a complaint about children's materials: I used my children as unpaid consultants. My daughter was four years old at the time. When I read her the book she looked at me and said, "That's a really silly book, Daddy."

There's something sad about a society where a four-year-old gets the joke, but a thirty-four-year-old doesn't.

Every children's book is not a moral fable or high-toned instruction manual, just as a Marx Brothers' movie is not a reliable guide to social etiquette.

Censorship Works

The most obviously false premise of censorship is that it works.

I have a friend in upstate New York. His library, like a sprinkling of libraries over a decade ago, bought *Show Me*—a sex education book that had some pictures of naked children.

His library, once upon a time, had two copies. One had long since disappeared. The other was quietly fading away in the obscurity of the back stacks, unused, forgotten, a month or so from becoming a victim of "weeding"—the removal of books no one wants.

But then a group with a name like "Parents of our Children" sprang up. Members wrote letters to the newspaper, demanding the instant removal of this perfidious example of child pornography. They rented trailers, pulling people in on one side and marching them past various tableaux: pictures from the book, over which a doleful grandmother cluck-clucked, and said, "Can you believe that?" And so on, until the hapless audience was dumped out the other end of the trailer thinking, "That's at the library?"

The result? First, the missing copy zoomed back to the shelf. No one wanted the shame of public exposure, especially when compounded with severe delinquency. After that, the complaints generated so much interest that the librarians had to do what they always do when the demand outstrips the supply: They bought more copies.

It is always so. "Banned in Boston" is the surest way to commercial success.

Complaining about a book publicly is likely to boomerang and greatly increase its availability and influence.

Removing a Book Makes a Library Better

A twist on another of the premises of censorship is that if removing a book makes a library better, then logically, the best library has no books at all.

When someone complains about a title that offends religious sensibilities, I remind them that one patron challenged the Bible on the basis that it was violent and contained references to rape, incest, and homosexuality. Should we toss out the Bible, too?

I got another challenge to the Bible. A gay man once pointed out to me that Leviticus clearly calls for the murder of men who lie with other men. Would I stock any other book that urged the populace to kill members of a minority?

Finally, which library is best? One that has few books, all in perfect agreement, or one that has many, even though some may be offensive . . . to someone?

The Premises of Literacy

In contrast to these premises, I offer the premises of democracy—and librarianship.

Literacy Is Better Than Illiteracy

Dobson is wrong. The reason we have so much crime is not that people are reading too much. It's that they can't read at all. Some 80 percent of today's prison population cannot read above the fourth-grade level.

Knowledge Is Better Than Ignorance

I could use the example of AIDS. Instead, let's use the Black Death. By conservative estimates, a third of the European populations died from this disease. While no one knew at the time what caused it, it was generally believed to be the judgment of a wrathful God.

What really caused the Black Death? Each household averaged one rat—and each rat averaged three fleas.

Knowledge is not only power, it is life.

Tolerance Is Better Than Intolerance

Community requires exposure to different views.

As I have come to know the people who have most directly attacked the library, I have learned to see them as individuals. Some are brighter than others, some more personable. On the whole, I like them. Some of them, to their surprise, found that they liked me, too. We have begun to break down that dangerous barrier of dehumanization.

How? As Woody Allen says, "Eighty percent of success is showing up." I attended CDCT meetings. When they talked about their kids, I talked about mine.

Naturally, many of these people suffer from the same myopia, ignorance, and suspicion as people at the other end of the religious and political spectrum. But that's what happens when you only read books you agree with, and only talk to people who share the same perspective.

If smug self-satisfaction and hostility are the illness—afflicting conservatives and liberals alike—why can't the library be the cure? Why not invite everybody to "read with the enemy"?

CHAPTER 3

Generations

I was in kindergarten, playing outside at recess. It was fall, and most of us were wearing jackets. Then I saw a couple of girls run screaming from Jimmy McLean.

Jimmy had tucked one of his jacket sleeves into its pocket. Then he pulled in his arm, stuck it down the inside of his jacket, and inside the front of his pants. Then he stuck his index finger out his fly and covered it with his other hand. He then walked up to the other kindergartners and said, "Wanna see something?" And he showed them his finger.

Well, I thought that was just about the funniest thing I'd ever seen. So I tried it. But before I got to the punch line, so to speak, I was collared by one of the recess monitors. She marched me into the principal's office. There, Jimmy and I got yelled at, trotted into the boy's rest room, whacked on the hind end a couple of times with a yardstick, and sent home.

When I arrived home, I was met by my father, who had been informed of the incident over the telephone. In some ways it was comical. "Do you have *any idea* what this means?" my father said, cupping a finger in his hand.

I did not.

"Do not *ever* do that again!" he thundered.

"OK," I said. And I hardly ever have.

This incident illustrates a couple of points. First, you never know what somebody is going to find funny. Especially grown-ups.

Second, it is almost impossible to imagine such a thing happening today. I experienced the complete uniformity of adult authority. The monitor, the principal, and my father acted as one.

Today there might be school psychologists gently investigating my emergent sexuality, neither the teacher nor the principal would have laid a hand on me, and everybody's parents would have consulted their attorneys.

I mentioned in the previous chapter my "Vanity of the Bonfires" speaking tour, in which I traveled around the county talking to various groups about the library and intellectual freedom. It was through these talks that I found out about Focus on the Family (FOF).

But I also made another discovery. My county has grown very rapidly. The areas that had grown the fastest were almost uniform in their demographics: white-collar professionals, well educated, between thirty-five and fifty years old, and white. But I didn't think much about that until I gave a presentation to a part of the county where there were a lot of older folks, mostly ranchers. To my surprise, this older generation was far more tolerant of alternative viewpoints. They were also indignant that some of these "yuppies" wanted to tell them what they couldn't read.

At that moment I realized there was a profound generational dynamic involved in censorship.

For a long time, I viewed the high number of challenges in our library as an anomaly, something that really didn't make sense, given the educational level of our patrons. Like many librarians, I equated the attempt to censor libraries as something more likely to happen in areas where people were poorly educated.

But there was another element: My most persistent challengers were members of my own generation, the Baby Boomers. What, I wondered, happened to the sixties?

But I realized the challenges didn't come despite our demographics, but because of them.

My father was a member of the GI generation. My mother was born on the cusp of the Silent generation. They backed authority. They were believers in "you can't fight city hall." If there was a conflict between authority and self, then authority won. That's not surprising, given that the defining experience of their lives was World War II, a time of massive social consensus and decisive action, all under a clear command structure.

By contrast, the driving philosophy of the sixties was "if there's a conflict between authority and my personal values, then authority has to change!" Most Boomers grew up believing that principled resistance to institutional authority—whether it be civil rights, the Vietnam War, or college curricula—was a strategy that worked. You *can* fight city hall, and what's more, you should.

That primacy of personal values over public institutions was not unique to the "counterculture." It also defines today's Boomer conservatives.

Today, we remember the Inquisition as the symbol of powerful and corrupt institutions, torturing the innocent to force them to renounce heresy, to give in to the all-powerful state and its thunderous values. But since the sixties, the United States has fostered another inquisition: that of the individual against the institution.

The New Inquisition is the legacy of the mid-life Baby Boomers, the belief that it is an urgent ethical mission to challenge, resist, even torture any public institution that crosses you. They believe the institution—particularly if tax-supported—is always wrong. This, of course, is as mistaken as the belief that it is always right.

Types and Life Cycles

According to historians William Strauss and Neil Howe (1997), and the web site www.fourthturning.com:

- There are four basic generational types. And here a generation means "a cohort sharing a moment in history, bound by key decisive experiences or events." People live through these experiences together, within the same phase of life: childhood, rising adulthood, mid-life, or elderhood. Generations vary in length, but average about twenty years.
- The generational types follow each other in strict sequence throughout U.S. history.
- Their alignment (relative phases of life) results in societal moods, called "turnings," that also follow a predictable sequence.
- Every two generations (at the second and fourth "turnings"), there is a crisis, either relating to an upheaval of values or a secular crisis.
- We are approaching the fourth turning and a secular crisis.

But let's start with the generational names, from the beginning of the last full cycle, to today:

- Missionary (Prophets), born 1860–1882
- Lost (Nomads), born 1883–1900
- GI (Heroes), born 1901–1924
- Silent (Artists), born 1924–1942
- Boomer (Prophets), born 1943–1960
- Gen-X (Nomads), born 1961–1981
- Millennial (Heroes), born 1981–present

These generational cohorts fit into four types, almost archetypes, whose lives tend to follow a broadly similar course.

Prophets (or Idealist): Indulged as youth, they are known for a coming-of-age passion, during which they challenge the dominant values of the day. In mid-life, they tend toward self-righteous moralism. They have the potential to become principled elder statesmen. They become increasingly protective as parents.

Nomads (or Reactive): Neglected, even abandoned as children, they become wild, risk-taking young adults. In mid-life, they become get-it-done survivalists. In their elder years, they tend to be suspicious and conservative. Reacting to their own childhoods, they tend to be overprotective as parents.

Heroes (or Civic): Protected as children, they become collaborative and disciplined soldiers as young adults. In mid-life, they tend toward hubris and arrogance. As elders, they are busy and social. They become increasingly indulgent as parents.

Artists (or Adaptive): Overprotected, even suffocated as children, they are conformist and quiet young adults. In mid-life, they serve as advisors, known for their flexible, consensus-building expertise. As elders, they continue to serve as intergenerational bridges. Again in reaction to their upbringing, they become underprotective as parents.

Finally, the four "turnings" of society go something like this:

First Turning: A "high," following the successful triumph over a secular crisis. Think post–World War II, with GIs returning to rising prosperity, strong social consensus, and the raising of hordes of children. This is a period of strengthening institutions and weakening individualism.

Second Turning: A passionate era of spiritual upheaval, when the civic order comes under attack from a new regime. The sixties.

Third Turning: An era of "malaise," of strengthening individualism and weakening institutions. The old civic order decays, and the new values advance. Think the end of the Carter presidency and the rise of the Reagan administration.

Fourth Turning: A decisive era of secular upheaval, when social consensus is rediscovered, and institutions are made anew. According to Strauss and Howe, we are nearing the cusp of this turning. In the book *Generations*, they even suggest an event that might be the trigger for such a turning: a terrorist attack.

Strauss and Howe's work in *Generations* is fascinating, not least because of the many predictions it made before Clinton's election—many of which have now come true. The book, of course, isn't astrology. Strauss and Howe observe a pattern and suggest that in broad outline, it might play out again. But history is dynamic, and not everyone will find themselves at ease, or in perfect congruence, with their generational profile.

Nonetheless, Strauss and Howe's work provides a framework for the analysis of current events.

For instance, we *did* face a terrorist attack. Yet, unlike the triggering effect of Pearl Harbor, 9/11 did not snap the citizens of the United States into decisive unity. Why? Because the generational alignment that has led to such decisive action was half-a-step off. In World War II we had Prophets in elderhood (FDR), Nomads in mid-life (Eisenhower), Heroes as rising adults (the GIs), and Artists as overprotected children at home. We had leaders who spoke with moral authority, executives who knew how to get things done, and brave and collaborative hands to get after it.

But right now, our elders are the process-sensitive Silent generation. The Boomers are still in their take-no-prisoners, uncompromising battle of values. The Gen-Xers are still honing their survivalist skills. The Millennials are a little too young. We remain a nation divided.

Incidentally, Strauss and Howe describe a period much like that: the Civil War, the most devastating war we have fought (certainly on a proportionate basis of casualties, and almost in absolute numbers). Then, as now, we were a fractious nation.

Or to put it another way, it isn't just events that drive history, it is society's response to those events. And one of the key factors determining that response is the mix of perspectives of the people in power—itself the result of generational mixes.

Now apply this model to intellectual freedom challenges. Why does my library get so many denunciatory challenges, when libraries in more demographically diverse communities get so few? Because my patrons fall squarely into the most moralistic and self-righteous time of the Prophets' (Boomers') life cycle.

And why do most of the challenges revolve around children's books and books for teenagers? Because the Prophets, and the Gen-Xers behind them, are more protective of their children and are growing overprotective.

These are the people who believe that in a conflict between private values and public purpose, the library must change immediately. Why? For the children.

I've been there myself.

Public Education: A Profile

I didn't set out to become an educational activist. I had almost entirely positive feelings about public education, in part because I had had a great experience myself, and in part because I count so many teachers among my friends.

Then, when my daughter, Maddy, was four years old, I found myself between a group of intense library-using mothers and a local elementary school principal. The moms had a series of concerns about their children's educations.

In brief, they were baffled and worried about the inability of their fourth- and fifth-graders to spell, do math, or write. One day, they were about to charge up to the local elementary school to confront the principal.

I volunteered to go along to moderate and facilitate. I thought it couldn't be that bad.

The contingent of four moms and me were politely admitted to the principal's office. He had a Ph.D., and made a point of being introduced as (let's call him) "Dr. Gomez."

I said, "I tagged along today because I've been listening to some of the comments of these parents, and I had some questions."

"Go ahead," said the good doctor. "I'm always happy to dialogue with the parents."

"Great," I said. "Here's my first question. Suppose that I've looked over the school curriculum. And I have—we have a copy of it for the library. And suppose I think that some areas of the curriculum need work. How would I go about trying to beef it up?"

Dr. Gomez frowned. "Well, we're on a curriculum review cycle of about seven years. It takes us that long to work through all the subject areas and incorporate new research. To my knowledge, parents have never been a part of that cycle. But I'd be happy to pass that idea along to district administration."

"Thanks," I said. "My next question concerns the teacher. Suppose the curriculum guide clearly states that the student know ... well, do you have a curriculum handy?"

Dr. Gomez excused himself, stepped into a closet, rummaged around for a while, and returned, blowing the dust from a big notebook. He handed it to me.

I found the section for fourth grade. At the end of the section it strongly suggested that by the end of the year, each child would be multiplying two numbers that were three digits apiece.

I read this aloud, and asked the parents of the fourth-graders if, since this was now the end of the year, their children knew how to multiply two three-digit numbers.

"No!" they exclaimed. "They haven't been taught anything about multiplication! That's why we're here!"

"And there's my question," I continued. "Suppose you have a teacher who simply isn't teaching to the curriculum?"

Dr. Gomez favored me with a warm and tolerant smile. "We would observe the teacher closely. And if this issue persisted across several semesters, we would intervene with continuing education and mentoring."

"I see," I said. "Now let's say you've got a teacher who is teaching to the curriculum, and doing a good job of it. But my daughter isn't getting it. My wife and I come in and talk to the teacher, and she gives us great advice and worksheets. We diligently work with our daughter, but now it's the end of the year, and Maddy just never understood this multiplication thing."

Again, I saw the wise smile, this time, with a touch of sympathy and reassurance. "We believe that it is very important to keep the child together with her peer group. We would move your daughter into the next grade, but be prepared to provide some additional tutoring."

"Ah," I said. "Now suppose it's the other way around. Now Maddy knows, on the first day of class, all about multiplication."

"Again, it's very important to keep the child with her peer group. We might also try to find some enrichment activities."

"Right. One last question. When I hire someone to shelve our books, I might spend forty-five minutes or so trying to make sure that the person is a good fit at the library. But the teacher of my daughter is even more important to me than a library shelver. Do I, as a parent, have the opportunity to interview the teacher before placing my daughter under his or her care?"

Now I got a knowing smile, yet firm. "We believe that we are the best qualified to determine the best academic environment for your child."

I stood up. "I have no further questions. Thank you for your time, Dr. Gomez."

As we filed out, I saw him send out an intern after me. She approached me, smiling. "What did you think of Dr. Gomez's answers?"

I stopped, then ticked off the points on my fingers. "I have no opportunity to influence what is taught. The teacher is not accountable for teaching anything. My child, whether she does poorly or well [two fingers], will be moved into the next grade. And finally, I have no say over who the teacher is." I shook my head.

"I would be insane to give you my child."

To his credit, Dr. Gomez did follow through on something called the Curriculum Advisory Committee, which included both parents and teachers. I attended it regularly for more than a year. In that time, we were presented with a number of documents, already in process.

While I genuinely liked most of the people involved, I couldn't help but notice that there was a distinct tone to these meetings. We were being lectured to, not listened to.

When the parents on the committee tried, and we did try, to get at some of the underlying issues, we were firmly steered back into educational process, where, of course, we were outsiders and amateurs.

I remember saying, "I don't want to tell teachers *how* to teach. That's their job, and I'm not trying to second-guess them. My concern is just *what* they teach. I'm not trying to judge process; I'm interested in the product, the thing I get the tax bill for."

I worked up and down several levels of the educational bureaucracy. And I found myself increasingly angered by this simple truth: I couldn't find anybody who could tell me what a child was supposed to know. (That earlier curriculum, and its clear expectations, were obviously no longer endorsed by the district.)

Equally frustrating was the fact that school administration officials kept changing their definition of their mission. (This was true not just locally but nationally. The school's job was to provide drug education through D.A.R.E. It was to provide sex education. It was to build character. It was to build responsible citizens. It was to feed the poor.) It encompassed, apparently, everything. In practice, this seemed to mean that it promised nothing. This diffusion and loss of mission is a potent lesson for libraries.

Finally, I walked out of a committee meeting. We had just been asked to give our approval to a new document, to be presented to the Board of Education. None of the things we had argued for were in the document, and many of the things we protested had been left in. It was a bald-faced attempt to co-opt us.

In the following months, I participated in the creation of the first parent-initiated charter school in Colorado. This process involved many, often contentious, public meetings. Over and over, I heard charter school proponents characterized as mean-spirited teacher bashers. Again and again, public officials refused to hear the core complaint.

Later, I even served twice on the charter school board. Sometimes, I found myself putting in some thirty hours a week for the school.

By the time my daughter turned five, my wife and I had made up our minds. We chose homeschooling. In thirty hours a week, you can do a pretty good job of teaching your kids.

About this time, the national trend toward content standards—in essence, the same issue many parents, and me among them, had been pushing—resulted in curricular changes. Despite early administrative protests that the curriculum could be altered only over the course of many years, in fact such changes, even sweeping changes, were easily and swiftly accomplished.

There's more to an educational institution than curriculum, of course, and many of those other factors are consistently ignored.

I would even argue that the current spate of educational reform has gone too far in its prescriptive nature. This excess is a consequence, I believe, of both sides saying, "All or nothing," to the detriment of our children. Administrators, teachers, and parents seem to have forgotten that not every child learns in the same way.

But there are now many schools in Colorado and many, many homeschoolers. And like many parents, my wife and I now sit down every year and review the options. What do we do this year? Homeschool? Charter school? Neighborhood school? Private school? (Eventually, both of our kids found their way to public schools. My daughter graduated from the local high school's International Baccalaureate program and is now in college overseas. My son is in middle school, after participating in an elementary school's gifted and talent program.)

My wife and I are getting a good education for our kids. We are knowledgeable education consumers. The school district now offers a variety of choices to the parent willing to dig for the information. It's a lot of work. But for many years, I rarely took anything an educator, particularly an administrator, told me for granted. That initial unresponsiveness of institutional leadership led to my persistent distrust of them.

On the other hand, I'm not angry about it anymore. I've matured—and I also understand the extent to which I got swept up in a movement and how my generational perspective ran away with me.

Let's review. First, the leadership of the public school patronized me. Then they tried to co-opt me. Then they attacked me. Then we had several nasty set-tos in public. Finally, we worked our way to a new balance.

What does all this have to do with public libraries?

As noted above, lots of Baby Boomer (and a smaller contingent of Gen-Xer) parents are inclined to put their own notion of their children's well-being ahead of any institutional goal. In itself, that's not bad and, in fact, may be an important part of the generational and historic dynamic: the revaluing of long-standing institutions. People have to be tested; so, too, do the organizations they build. Organizations, like people, can grow out of touch, arrogant, and unresponsive. This serves no one.

We are still in a period of the New Inquisition, of the radical re-examination of public institutions. First, it was public schools. In more recent years (as seen both in lawsuits in Livermore, California, and Loudon County, Virginia, and in the growth of new groups such as Virginia's Family Friendly Libraries and FOF), it has been public libraries.

These people have asked three questions. First, what does the institution really stand for? Second, how closely does this publicly funded institution match my own values and expectations for society? Third, how do the people who run that institution treat me when I ask these questions?

I learned from my encounters with the school district that the way an institution responds is not trivial. It has a profound effect on future interactions and outcomes. After all, I myself went from a placid taxpayer and a modest school booster to a virulently outspoken opponent of a proposed bond issue. Then I actively set about working to create alternatives. The fact that several trends have swept the country—charter schools, homeschooling, standards, testing, vouchers, and an alarming exodus of qualified teachers into other fields—speaks to the power and the danger of sudden movements.

It could happen to libraries. It will happen unless librarians learn to talk—and more importantly, to listen—to their critics.

Focus on the Family: Redefining the Mission

The August 2004 issue of FOF's *Citizen* magazine featured an article called "Danger Zone." The subtitle read, "Think it's safe to leave your kids alone at the library? Think again."

It began with a scare story. Earlier that year, a homeless man came to the Philadelphia Free Library, where he "allegedly" (we don't know by whom) made a habit of looking at pornography. There, in one of the rest rooms, he beat and raped an unattended eight-year-old girl.

The author then stated that "safety isn't an issue just in Philadelphia. Libraries across the nation have, as of July 1, implemented measures promoted by a new federal law designed to reduce the chances of a similar attack occurring elsewhere: The Children's Internet Protection Act

(CIPA) requires all libraries wishing to receive federal funds to install filters that will prevent not only children but adults, from downloading
pornography."

Child abuse is indeed a serious problem in America. I once served on
the board of an organization that dealt with survivors of child abuse, and
it continues to haunt me. Just for the record, though, overwhelming
research shows that the most dangerous place for a child is *not* a library.
It's home. Most child abuse is perpetrated by immediate relatives. By family. That's a point that an organization calling itself "Focus on the Family"
fails to focus on.

But what's really going on here? In brief, it's the attempt to redefine
the mission of the public library, to reframe the debate. To the author of
the article, the idea is that "my personal value of 'safety' means preservation not only of physical freedom from attack, but the preservation of an
environment where no child can gain access to information about
sexuality." Then this personal statement of values is projected onto the
public library.

But, of course, this is not the mission of the library. What is that
mission?

- To gather
- To organize
- To publicly present the intellectual resources of our culture

In brief, our job is not to "protect" a child by ensuring his or her ignorance. Indeed, knowledge is a better defense.

This doesn't mean that public space is entirely unsupervised. Nor
does it mean that everything available in the library is either of interest
to, or appropriate for, an elementary school student. It does mean that
various services—such as Internet access—will be first tested against this
primary mission.

But librarians need to be careful here. While it is necessary to clearly
state our purpose in public life, it is not sufficient to respond to all
challenges.

There is a question behind the question. A concerned parent who
read the *Citizen* article might well ask, "So does anything go at the library
these days? Any books? Any magazines? Any web pages? Any kind of
patron behavior? What is your library doing to ensure that children are
safe and offered things appropriate to their age?" That's a reasonable
question.

And it's the *real* question. If we dodge it by hiding behind policies
and jargon, we will reap the same mistrust sown by the educational establishment of the early nineties.

Anything Goes?

The short answer is no. Societies have laws; libraries have policies. There are limits to what can be considered acceptable behavior.

And like laws, policies mostly spell out what our patrons are *not* allowed to do. Some of these things are so painfully obvious that sometimes just having to set them to paper seems insulting. But like those companies compelled to put absurd warnings on their products (Warning: This gasoline is not to be taken internally; do not insert this screwdriver into your nose, etc.), we sometimes have to call out those things people consistently get wrong.

The core policy for a library tends to be its "materials selection." This tends to be broadly construed, alarmingly so to many concerned parents. But that overlooks something. Libraries are generally organized according to the patterns of probable use. That is, children's departments are stocked with materials that have been demonstrated—by use or format— to be of interest to children. Adult collections tend *not* to be of significant appeal to children. It all may be "available," but it isn't of interest to everybody. There is a natural boundary in what people are looking for.

Libraries typically adopt other policies as well. We try to describe what falls outside the limits of behavior in a public place. Since the Internet, even before the imposition of filtering, we lay out some guidelines.

Nonetheless, laws are broken. Library policies are broken. Sometimes people get away with it. Sometimes we catch them. In this, libraries are no different than any other social network.

Acceptable Behavior

In general, most libraries expect that our patrons will be both law-abiding and civil. Sometimes, this faith is touchingly naive. Most patrons understand that not only is it inappropriate to commit a crime in our buildings, but also that library patrons are typically seeking the quiet enjoyment of the premises. But there are others who believe that their own children are above such restrictions, or imagine that since they are taxpayers, they may use publicly funded facilities precisely as they please. This attitude is as ill-informed as it is discourteous.

Libraries have taken various approaches to establishing acceptable behavior policies. I'm inclined to go with the broadest, most inclusive language, as in "patrons will be both law-abiding and civil." However, a policy should reflect local conditions, and should involve public review and probably the oversight of an attorney.

Internet Use by Minors

Like most public libraries in this country, my library is governed by lay citizens. We have discussed, at great length and on several occasions, our role in the use of the Internet by minors.

I should emphasize that "minors" is an elastic term, typically encompassing everyone age 17 and under. In practice, minors fall into at least three distinct categories.

1. **Preschool and preliterate:** No one of this age should be using the Internet alone.

2. **Elementary age:** This has some stretch to it. Generally, these are children still young enough to not be particularly interested in sex, although they may indeed be interested in the violent action of various video games. There are definitely Internet sites of interest to this age group. Few librarians object to the use of software filters for this group, guarding against the occasional mistyping of a web address or the accidental subject hit ("spanking" as in the corporal punishment of children as opposed to light S&M between consenting adults).

3. **'Tween and teen:** At this point, "minors" are starting to show distinct interest in adult subjects. They are curious about sex. They want to know more about drugs and other controlled substances. They have started to investigate the extremes of human conduct.

In my experience, most of the emotion around this topic concerns those minors in 'tween and teen category.

Do libraries care about these children? Indeed we do, and we demonstrate this concern in a variety of ways.

1. **Selection and presentation:** We direct minors to positive, high-quality sites, created or reviewed by librarians.

2. **Instruction:** Libraries offer classes that teach parents and children how to search the World Wide Web safely and effectively.

3. **Interior design:** We often place Internet workstations, wherever possible, in direct view of our staff so the space can be easily supervised. This also serves a second purpose of enabling staff to determine whether someone needs assistance.

4. **Filters or Internet protection measures:** In some states, such filters are required or have been installed so the library can receive federal funds.

5. **Investigation of complaints:** If one patron claims to be disturbed or offended by another's use of the Internet, staff will investigate. A range of options is possible: The use may be perfectly innocuous and allowed to continue. The use may be observably illegal—child pornography, for instance—in which case staff will intervene or contact authorities, depending on local procedure.

6. **Postings:** To address issues of safety and security of minors when using electronic mail, chat rooms, and other forms of electronic communication, the library may post information urging minors to follow basic safety guidelines: Never give out personal information (name, address, phone number, etc.), never arrange via a computer to meet someone, never respond to messages

that are threatening or suggestive, and remember that people online may not be who they say they are.

7. **Supervision of public space:** Minors, like adults, are expected to behave in a civil and appropriate manner in the library. The display of visual material that is sexual in nature or that might be considered immediately offensive to others constitutes rude behavior. In such circumstances, at the discretion of library staff, patrons will be asked to cease such behavior. If they do not, they may be ejected from the library, and risk the loss of future library privileges.

Enforcement and Consequences

No one, minor or adult, has the right to use public property to commit crimes. At the same time, no policy can ensure that crimes will never be committed. If library patrons are found to be accessing materials that may be, at the discretion of library staff, obscene or illegal, they can be ejected from the library and may be barred from future use of library resources. Again, such a policy, and consequent procedures, should be thoughtfully constructed and reviewed.

Is It Enough?

Usually, all of the above is sufficient to ensure a comfortable and productive library environment. However, there are circumstances in which even the most thoughtful policy framework, consistent staff training, and intelligently delivered staff interpretation will fail.

This is where we find the fault line between legitimate concern about the public library and the hysteria of alarmist attacks. Libraries *should* think about such issues and prepare for them. The World Wide Web did indeed greatly broaden the kind and type of material that could be accessed in the library, utterly bypassing even the broadest librarian review.

But by and large, libraries have done an excellent job of addressing this issue.

I have to conclude this section with a true story. One late afternoon, a librarian at a neighboring district stepped out of the staff room to see a middle-aged woman sitting next to a fifteen-year-old boy. Each of them was using an Internet workstation.

The librarian was surprised to see a graphic sexual image on the boy's screen, so surprised that she reacted without thinking: She screamed. The middle-aged woman sitting next to the boy then looked at the screen. She screamed, too.

Then the woman turned angrily to the librarian. "How *dare* you," she sputtered, "let my son look at that in the library?"

Permit me a generational observation. If that had been *my* mother, it wouldn't have been the library that took the blame.

CHAPTER 4

Responding to Challenges

In this chapter, I'd like to do two things: first, be more specific about who is challenging library materials. Second, I hope to describe specific steps librarians should follow to respond to these challenges.

Before I get into either of those issues, however, let me make one point very clear: *In general, the response to a challenge should be handled by the library staff.*

It's likely that board members will receive complaints. But rather than trying to argue it through right on the spot, they should refer the challenge to staff. That might mean offering to get a "reconsideration" form for the person registering the complaint or having a staff member call him or her.

It is important that the board member retain objectivity for the final appeal. This also applies to other non-board supervisors of librarians. When higher-ups step around the process, there is one reliable result: Materials get pulled and services are eliminated, often without thoughtful consideration or dialogue.

Who Are They?

Who are the people who challenge libraries?

Something approaching 98 percent of all the challenges I receive come from people in one of two categories:

1. The parents of children between the ages of four and six
2. The parents of children between the ages of fourteen and sixteen

The End of Infancy

I have two children myself, and I do understand.

In the first blush of parenthood, I was absorbed with and charmed by my daughter. I quickly learned all those habits of protectiveness—moving the drinking glasses away from the edge of the dinner table, holding her hand when we crossed the street, snatching her up when I saw a loose dog.

At about the age of four, children begin interacting with the world in a way that's less physical and more concerned with language and social behavior. It's about this time that parents start cleaning up their own language and being annoyed by their childless friends, who swear no more than they always had.

The idyll of infancy has come to a close. Parents begin to see that the dangers of the world are both larger and less well defined than the hazards of broken glass, speeding cars, and big dogs. Often, parents reach this realization ... at the library.

Consider the story of the Buddha, once Prince Gautama. Gautama's father sought to protect his son from any knowledge of the world's suffering. The young Gautama was not to see illness, poverty, or death. Eventually, however, driven by urges he did not understand and could not control, Gautama encountered the world's ills anyway. In his shock and horror, he did just what his father feared: The child abandoned his family, fleeing pell-mell to his own, independent future.

Until their children reach the age of four or so, parents feel that the world is controllable; they can create and maintain a generally safe environment. But library collections, even in the children's room, provide ample evidence of the world's woes. No matter that you have told your child that it's not nice to call anyone names. One day, your child picks up a book of insults and finds it hilarious. Or you're working hard to have your child be neat and tidy—then she falls in love with a book about a happy slob.

So many of the challenges libraries receive have an emotional content that seems, at first, puzzling and disproportionate. Why? Because parents have just realized that the world is not controllable, that there are a wide range of influences in the world that are exactly contrary to the messages they want to send their children.

Thus such parents' first reaction is a kind of stunned anger. Why are you, a public institution paid for by tax dollars, deliberately sabotaging their conscientious parenting?

It is often their own dedication that leads some parents to crusades and blinds them to their own arrogance. They volunteer to review every book in the children's area because librarians clearly don't understand the effect of literature on young minds. Out with all of the disturbing influences! In with innocuous literature, like ... the Berenstain Bears!

Eventually, most parents resign or adjust. By then, their children are off in public schools, and the library isn't quite the threat it used to be. Now the dangers are TV, peer pressure, the lessons of soccer sportsmanship, and how to dress your child so he or she won't be publicly belittled. Parents may even learn a new respect for librarians and even welcome their skills at matching personalities to genres. The library becomes again what it was at the beginning: a social asset.

The Wonder Years

The next crisis point comes with puberty. Suddenly, your children don't even look like children anymore. They're taller than you are. They have breasts and body hair. You begin to notice all the teenagers with driver's licenses. You remember all too clearly the night you borrowed your father's car and crossed a distant state line for purposes that, even then, you knew were questionable.

Then there's the age-old irony of battling generational sensibilities. Just as you're settling into a period of maximum conservatism (you are, after all, saving for college and retirement), your children enter their period of maximum radicalism. They start questioning everything.

They stop going to church, or they go to churches with beliefs that baffle you.

They take drugs. Your children could go to jail, or get shot, or overdose.

They have sex. Your son has grown furtive, your daughter brazen. The holding pattern of adolescence is breaking up, and there are a host of new worries: pregnancy, disease, licentiousness. Just when you long to wrap your children back in swaddling clothes, to pull them closer, you realize they are drawn instead to other, wilder arms.

Despite all the hype about Internet pornography, two of the three challenges I've gotten based on real circumstances involved fifteen-year-old boys, caught in the act of investigation by their fathers. One exasperated father banged his fist on my desk and said, "I caught my son looking at girlie pictures on your library's computers!"

"Tell him to stop," I said. "We don't appreciate that kind of behavior here, and that's not why we bought those computers."

It stopped him cold. And I could see his deep despair—"The library can't control him either." He left, defeated.

And it's true, we can't control his son, other than in the grossest sense by monitoring detectable violations of courtesy and law. We can oversee, remonstrate, attempt to redirect, and exile. And we do. But that's all we can do. Institutions assist in the process of promoting general social stability, but they, like parents, always have people probing the boundaries.

Eventually, of course, parents make another adjustment. They negotiate new limits and define new consequences. They try to find a new way to communicate with these suddenly strange beings, these changelings. Parents find themselves, again, reflecting that there are no shortcuts to experience. Control is an illusion. There is only love, and longing, and perhaps the faint whisper of early influence.

And there is the most profound grief.

Buddha is at the gate, running.

Good News about Parents

Yet there is much good news about this observation concerning the typical source of intellectual freedom challenges.

First, the parents use the library. They value literacy.

Second, they brought their kids to see us. And their children use the library, too.

Third, these parents actually pay attention to and care about their children's library use.

Fourth, the parents typically have a very clear sense of their values and are working hard to communicate those values to their offspring.

Fifth, they have taken the time, inconvenient and uncomfortable as that might be, to talk directly to decision makers in public institutions about one of the core services of that institution: the quality and composition of the collection.

All of these things are rarer than they should be. The library should encourage, not punish, such behavior. To put it another way, the library should value these individuals. They are among the best building blocks we have for community support—providing, of course, that we take them seriously, that we provide materials of use to them, and that we maintain service standards that reflect our mission and purpose in public life.

We must not, we cannot, view them with contempt.

The Initial Response

Someone has complained to you about some library material or service.

The complaint—a challenge—comes to you in one of several ways. It could be in person, over the phone, or in writing (paper or e-mail).

Each of these has its own strategies. A personal, face-to-face contact is the most demanding, but may also be the most powerful. Here, it's not just what you say, it's a host of other behaviors. When receiving a complaint in person, maintain an open posture (not an arms-crossed defensive huddle), make eye contact, and stay alert and respectful. Your voice should be clear and even.

If the complaint comes over the phone, you may be able to pace, if that helps you think. You can close your eyes or doodle or make notes. But again, you must speak clearly and cogently.

If the complaint is in writing, you can try out various responses and be more thoughtful. This last may be the reason many libraries have policies requiring a complaint to be in writing.

But however the challenge arrives, there are some fairly simple rules to follow when dealing with an initial complaint.

Rule No. 1: Apologize

In general, people don't complain just for the fun of it. Taking the time to notify an institution of a problem often involves personal discomfort on the part of the person doing the complaining. It is inconvenient. Quite often, there is an emotional component to the challenge. In the back of their minds, the people complaining know they might lose it— i.e., start shouting, get teary, meet hostility, or worse. That knowledge may make them even more on edge.

In these litigious times, many of us are reluctant to express any sympathy, lest it be turned into an admission of guilt. Nonetheless, I believe a simple apology is both appropriate and polite. Say, "I'm sorry!" and mean it. You're sorry that they had so unpleasant an experience that it upset them. Before you is a human being who may be facing a difficult thing. Be kind.

Rule No. 2: Don't Be Defensive; Listen

The most common mistake made by library staff is becoming wildly defensive. There is nothing inherently aggressive about differences in opinion. If someone says to you, "I like malts," and you happen to prefer milkshakes, you probably aren't driven to trot out anti-malt manifestos or cite the Citizens for a Fair Shake foundational documents. If a library patron were to say, "I hate this carpet color," you probably wouldn't take it personally. You might agree, disagree, or have no opinion one way or the other, and just make a polite reply.

The same is true of challenges. Someone is expressing an opinion. That's an interesting thing and may contain valuable information regarding the public perception of your institution. Your job is not to silence the speaker, but to pay attention.

Ask, "What is your concern?"

Rule No. 3: Restate the Problem

After you've listened to the patron, restate the problem back to him or her until the patron agrees that you understand. Again, people raising challenges may be emotionally riled up and subsequently have difficulty communicating. A simple model for communication is one person who says, "I'm sending a message. Do you copy?" and another person saying,

"I copy." The second half of listening, and the key next step for library staff, is repeating or restating the message.

That message will vary. Based on my experience, it's likely to be some variety of "this is inappropriate for children." The specific concern may be expressed directly: "This book is about a homosexual relationship and for the library to have this book is to promote something God expressly forbids. To have it available for children is unconscionable."

It may be less specific: "This book is about those people."

It may be nonspecific: "I can't believe the library bought this garbage."

The mission of library staff is to clarify the concern, make it specific. It is not to prejudge that concern, defend library principles or practices, or to change the patron's mind. It is simply to understand the nature of the complaint.

When the complaint is not clear, it is best to begin by asking questions. Ask, "The book is about what people?" Keep asking questions until you understand.

When the case is stated clearly, library staff should say, "Your concern, then, is that this book is about a subject—homosexuality—that you believe should not be placed in the children's section." Then wait to get that restatement validated by a nod or a "yes, exactly."

Recognize that during this process, the patron may go off on tangents—"Libraries are packed with liberals, promoting all kinds of sexual content!" Avoid getting dragged into a rant. Instead, try to pull the patron back to the issue. Smile, and say, "I'm sorry, is it this book that concerns you? How come?"

There are people, of course, who can carry on all day no matter what you do. But most folks find it hard to stay mad when they're looking into an open, attentive, polite face, particularly when that person is clearly and sympathetically trying to get the point.

The task of library staff members is to stay focused and stay polite. You may not be able to be calm inside—your palms may sweat and your heart may be knocking—but it helps to put yourself in recorder mode. You're gathering a message for the library, and you want to make sure you get it right, that you "copy" the sender.

Very often, after hearing that the library staff member understands the nature of the concern, the patron will be satisfied. They've had their say; someone got it. That clears the deck for the next step.

Rule No. 4: Offer Service

Once you understand the problem, offer alternatives. In the case of the book on homosexuality in the children's room (*Daddy's Roommate*, by Michael Wilhoite, for instance), say, "Can I help you find something else for your child?" Or the question might be, "Were you looking for something in particular?"

This might put the patron right back into the rant. "Well, I wasn't looking for this!" An appropriate response might be, "No, I understand! But what were you looking for?" This opens a dialogue that might move to, "What sort of books does your child most enjoy?"

The underlying assumption of this exchange is that the patron came to the library seeking service and instead found something upsetting. After expressing the concern, the patron is presumably still interested in what brought him or her there to begin with. The goal of the library staff is to have patrons walk out with something that satisfies their library need, a positive service transaction.

Rule No. 5: Offer Follow-up if Advised

Despite your best efforts, however, and even if you succeed in providing a book the patron is pleased with, the patron may want to pursue the original concern further. How will you know?

He or she will tell you. The subject will be reopened, perhaps with questions such as, "Who orders these books?" It might be more direct: "I'd like to do something about this book."

In the case of questions, you should respond as you would to any other reference question: Give accurate information. If the patron clearly is seeking some further action, then pass them quickly to the next step.

That may vary according to local library policy. In some cases, that might mean (or the patron might request) speaking with someone higher up the supervisory ladder—a supervisor, department head, or director.

In other cases, it might be presenting the patron with some kind of form. This form can be generic (a suggestion box form) or specific to library materials ("Request for Reconsideration"). Most reconsideration forms are fairly straightforward: They seek to ascertain the date the challenge was received, by whom, who issued the complaint, and the nature of the concern. In the sample below, I have also included some questions that might be useful to building the collection.

Using the Form

In general, I have found that it's not a good idea to ask what the patron thinks should be done with the challenged item or service. For instance, I don't recommend asking if the patron wants to get rid of a book, have it reclassified, or have it put in some special collection (the infamous locked case of library lore). If the complaint concerns a library service or display, other options may be available. On occasion, the patron makes such a request or suggestion on his or her own.

To my mind, the value of the reconsideration form is in gathering relevant information from the challenger and facilitating the review of the

Sample Request for Reconsideration Form

Title: _____

Author: _____

Location: _____

Date request received by staff: _____ Staff initials: _____

Type of material: [ ] Book [ ] Audiotape [ ] Video [ ] Magazine/newspaper [ ]
Art [ ] Other

Request initiated by: _____
Signature: _____

Mailing address: _____

Telephone: ( ) _____

Representing: [ ] Self [ ] Organization

Organization address: _____

Phone: ( ) _____

What concerns you about this material? Please be specific. Cite pages.

Did you read/listen to the entire item? If no, what parts?

What do you believe is the central theme of this material?

Is there any age group for which this material might be appropriate? If so,
please specify.

Are there, in your judgment, any positive elements in this material? Please
describe.

Are you aware of any literary reviews of this material? (If so, please cite.)

What material(s) can you suggest to counterbalance the point of view of
this material or provide additional information on the subject?

item. The disposition of the item remains a professional decision, and it's hard to anticipate the precise resolution.

After having given patrons the form, collect it, thank them for taking the time to express their concern, and assure them that a timely response will be forthcoming.

Rule No. 6: Follow Up

The brief explanation of this rule: Follow your procedures. The formal, written challenge marks the beginning of a process. That process involves, at a minimum, the review by a committee or assigned staff member(s) of the complaint and the item or service in question and notification of the complainant of any decision, as well as placing that decision within a policy framework. Clearly, this process is only necessary when you have contact information for the person complaining. It doesn't make sense, in most cases, to go through a formal process to follow up on anonymous material complaints. On the other hand, staff is likely to investigate the more shocking allegations regardless of whether the complainant is identified (For example, "This children's book has graphic photographs of bestiality!" No, it didn't, graphic or otherwise.)

Timeliness is important in this stage. If the process takes a subjectively long time—five or six weeks—then a letter should go out the first week to explain the process, and how long it might be before the patron hears back from the library regarding the matter.

Also of great importance is including all relevant library policies. People actually take notice when you attach internal guidelines. It demonstrates that the institution has considered both principles and standards. It declares what the institution stands for, removing it from a mere personal conflict, one opinion against another.

Most of the time, alas, the library will not do precisely what the complainant is seeking. While I have withdrawn several books people have complained about (on the basis of age and condition, rather than content), that's rare. For some members of the public, that means that the library is unresponsive.

But responsiveness doesn't mean appeasement or agreement. It means that something happens. In the case of reconsideration, the library is obligated to take a thorough, thoughtful look at the item or service being challenged and to communicate that process, the decision, and the reasoning behind it, as promptly as possible.

As I previously noted, I have written almost two hundred letters to patrons seeking reconsideration of library materials. When I encounter these people later, they often say something like, "I appreciated your response. I didn't agree with you, but I could tell you listened, and you thought about it, and you got back to me." They also seem to be particularly impressed that the letter came from a person, not a committee.

Finally, follow-up is a balance of personal and institutional: personal courtesy and institutional consistency to mission and process.

Other Tips

Remember to be human. You don't have to like everything in the library, and it's OK to say so. Once I saw a patron slam a book on the circulation counter and declaim, "This book is awful!" The circulation clerk reached behind her and grabbed a best-seller from the hold shelf. She slammed it down beside the other book. "Yes," she said, disgusted. "And this one is even worse! What is it with these publishers?" Five minutes later, patron and staff member had bonded: They shared a deep disapproval of book publishing today. Then, and now, I found it a brilliant technique for disarming potential institutional critics. Some books truly are awful. Why not admit it? Why not set aside policy and talk to the patron with the unfiltered frankness of the typically well-read library staff person?

Note, however, that once the patron moves to a specific request to pull the book, library staff has to make the transition from chum to employee. That transition may be difficult. When the patron says, "Don't you think the library should get rid of this?" the staff member needs to be able to speak to the library's mission. He or she might say, "You know, there are lots of books I don't agree with. But there are many more that I love. Have you tried ... ?" Again, the intent is to move the patron to a successful transaction and perhaps to underscore that the great value of the library is not what it doesn't have, but what it does.

Avoid institutional arrogance. The most precious, hard-to-come-by information is why people are dissatisfied with your service. Use the encounter to probe perceptions of your institution. Are you living up to your mission? In an earlier chapter, I included some correspondence between my library and the Church of Jesus Christ of Latter-Day Saints. The initial complaint was about a video that church officials found offensive. One of my findings was that my library, in fact, had a very negative and slanted collection about Mormonism. Such things happen, but when the bias is called to your attention, you're obligated to correct it and to thank the person or people who called the matter to your attention.

The Written Responses: Letters

This section focuses on the usual result of a reconsideration process: a letter that goes to the person who issued the challenge.

There are general categories of public concerns. The Colorado State Library, in response to a perceived jump in challenges a few years ago, now routinely collects statistics from state public libraries. Objections to library materials tend to fall into the following categories (and at least in 2000, in the following order):

- Unsuited to age group
- Sexually explicit
- Homosexuality
- Nudity
- Religious viewpoint
- Occult
- Satanism
- Offensive language
- Violence
- Drugs
- Racism
- Political viewpoint

While every item or service being challenged has its own idiosyncrasies, circumstances, and personality, I can recommend a general format for a response. I don't always follow it myself, at least not in this order, but I do try to include all of the elements.

Policies

Make sure you attach a copy of your policies, including at least the Library Bill of Rights, the Right to Read statement, Collection Development, and Request for Reconsideration. There was one time—because the complaint came in as a more casual note rather than as a formal "request for reconsideration"—when I responded in writing, but did not send our policies. That resulted in the one of two times when the patron appealed my decision. I learned my lesson: Policies matter. They provide evidence that the library has carefully thought about what it does and why. They provide a context and framework for a decision. Have them, talk about them with the board and staff, and make sure you distribute them to the people complaining to you.

Thank You

Begin by thanking the patron. I often use some variation of "Thank you for taking the time to let me know your thoughts on this item. As a librarian with two children of my own, I very much appreciate someone who thinks about what a library has to offer and is willing to share those thoughts with us. It's rarer than you might think."

Restatement of Concern

Repeat, using the written statement, your understanding of the concern or concerns. This also reminds the patron of what he or she previously stated.

Response to Issues

This is the heart of the letter. Respond to the issues raised by the patron. I often find, particularly with children's materials, that there are two issues—one stated and one implied. First is the specific title; second is the larger concern of why such subjects are acquired for the children's area. In other words, people aren't just asking, "Why do you have this book?" They're saying that they have expectations about what they'll find in the children's library, and they don't understand why the library violates that expectation.

In other cases, the second issue may be something different. The point is to grapple with what the complaint is really about. As you'll see in the Appendix, I typically explain that material in the children's area is put there not because of the topic but because of general format—the many things that add up to "intended for children," such as length, use of pictures, and so on.

The Role of the Library

Usually as a part of the response, I make a statement about the underlying philosophy of library service. This is my opportunity to clarify what the library stands for, to give a context for the next step.

Action to Be Taken

Sometimes I put this early in the letter; more often, I place it near the end, after I have gone through my analysis. This is the communication of the decision: what change of status, if any, will occur. For most library materials, the choices are as follows:

- Buy additional copies, either at the same place, or in multiple locations. On occasion, I find a book so good that I add copies for other branches. Sometimes, too, I find that a book might fall easily into more than one category—both young adult and adult—and I have no problem with putting it in both locations, and thereby helping more than one audience find the book.
- Retain the title, as classified, at its current location.
- Retain the title, reclassified, at a new location (i.e., recatalog from children's to parenting collection, or children's to young adult, or young adult to adult, or adult to reference).

- Retain the title, but add materials to tell another side of the story.
- Withdraw the book. I've done this three times in sixteen years. On the basis of content, I've defended the books. But all three of them were beaten up and dated. Most libraries try to remove such materials as a matter of regular pruning. It seems hypocritical to keep something just because somebody complained about it, when you should have gotten rid of it anyway. I couldn't replace them, either, because they were all out of print. But we did buy other books on the same general topics (dating for teens, religious cults, and home decorating—a patron had complained about some sixties-style sexual posters shown in one of the illustrations for bedroom decorating).

Patrons frequently request two other kinds of changes. The first is to affix a warning label of some kind. My usual response is to indicate that the item has already been labeled through the process of cataloging. Adult books are labeled one way; children's books are labeled another. Children's videos are labeled differently than adult videos. In addition, labels often obscure information that is more specific and useful to the patron: the blurbs on audiotape packages and videos, for example.

On the other hand, one time I did agree with the patron that the title of a DVD (*Angels in America*) sounded like an acceptable family film. In fact, it was an adult drama about AIDS. The DVD case was largely blank and gave no indication of its content. I elected to add a label indicating that the movie contained adult language and situations. I recognize that the ALA has taken a stand against labeling. On the other hand, such a description is not pejorative, but descriptive. It simply assists the public in making good decisions about their selections when the existing packaging, cataloging, or placement in the collection is ambiguous or incomplete.

The other frequent patron request is to block the circulation of an item based on the age of the patron. Most often this concerns R-rated movies, which many people seem to feel is a federal mandate regulating what minors may view. Ratings, of course, don't have any legal authority at all; they are voluntary and somewhat arbitrary labels adopted by the Motion Picture Association of America.

I once got together with a friend of mine, another library director, who used the same circulation system we did. In the space of an afternoon, we worked up a complex matrix of patron and item priority levels that would permit each parent to work through a grid of choices, automatically restricting what their child's card would check out.

But neither of us ever adopted the system. Why? For one thing, the issue frankly doesn't come up often enough to justify the extra staff time and patron paperwork. For another, there's a lower-tech response: Parents can simply tell their children what's off limits and hold them accountable for any violations.

Possibility of Appeal

The penultimate thing is to say what the patron can do if he or she disagrees with the decision: In my case, that's an appeal to the board of trustees, "whose decision is final." This may vary, of course, according to your policies.

Thank You, Again

Close with a second expression of gratitude. This completes the cycle of courteous respect.

The Importance of Tone

Perhaps more important than the content checklist is tone. The greatest danger is falling into the jargon of our profession. The public perceives professional double-talk as condescension. This perception is often correct.

Resist the temptation to score debate points. You're not trying to win the argument; you're trying to win the patron. Library staff members are likely to live in the same communities as their patrons. Be ready to meet them again, look them in the eye, and know you did your best.

I've found it useful to run my draft letters past another staff person, preferably someone who isn't a librarian. I ask these questions: Is this clear? Is it courteous? The second read also helps catch typos.

Some librarians make it a point to dig up other reviews of a title. I've done it, too, on occasion, when I'm tracking down the reputation of an author or trying to get some sense of its target market. For many librarians, the search for reviews is an appeal to authority. It might explain why you bought something. Nonetheless, there's no substitute for your own judgment. Reviewers aren't necessarily any more insightful than anyone else.

While this can be risky, I also try to hit a human note. If it's a children's book, I let my kids look at it and tell the patron that I've done so. If a book or video seems to me to be in bad taste, I say so.

On occasion, I also cite the circulation statistics for an item. While they're not always a reliable indicator of value, they can be helpful in getting a read on general demand.

Samples in Appendix

I have placed representative samples of my patron letters in the Appendix. There you will find more detailed examples and explanations of the items above.

When the Issue Doesn't Die

It would be nice to think that the response process outlined above would bring about the end of a matter. In my case, overwhelmingly, that has been true.

But recently, one of my patrons did take a challenge all the way to a board appeal. My board president, who had a lot of experience managing public hearings for the county planning commission, set out a very clear process for conducting the appeal. It's worth sharing.

First, here was the complaint.

The book was *Princess Buttercup*, written by Wendy Cheyette Lewison and illustrated by Jerry Smath. It was about a group of fairies—diminutive but wingless beings, all female—planning a summer party. Princess Buttercup set out to gather honey for the party, then got distracted and lost. Eventually, she flagged down a butterfly and found her way back.

That's pretty much the whole story—a slice of the whimsical social life of mythical creatures.

But on one page appeared three lines about another fairy, Princess Iris. Iris was lazy. She didn't like to work. She liked to play ball. There was an illustration of Iris throwing a tiny blue ball into a spider web.

Oh, and one other thing. Alone among the fairies, Iris had brown skin and black, curly hair. Iris was a fairy of color.

The patron complaint was that this illustration, taken with the comments, promoted a dangerous and negative stereotype. It linked "laziness" with "black" with "basketball." No other fairy was so singled out for criticism.

The patron, who in addition to being thoughtful and articulate, was also a person of color, asked that we remove the book.

I reviewed the title and saw how the patron came to that conclusion. The description of Iris did seem gratuitous. On the other hand, it might have been the author or illustrator trying—if not succeeding—to be funny. The book was well used, the authors did not have a reputation for being insensitive to cultural diversity, and the "offense" might not have been intentional. I decided to keep the book. But I also wrote to the author, in care of the publisher, to tell her about the complaint and ask for her side of it.

I never received a response, even after a follow-up phone call.

The patron appealed my decision and was placed at the top of our agenda. (That's the first thing I'd suggest. If someone shows up to talk to you, get them as close to the beginning of your meeting as possible. Don't make them sit and simmer through a long session.)

An Appeals Process Outline

Basically, the process for an appeal should work something like this:

1. The board president opens a public hearing for the purposes of considering an appeal. The president summarizes our reconsideration policies (previously distributed to the board for review).

2. Staff summarizes the original reconsideration request and reasons for the library director's subsequent decision to retain material in the collection (in my case, the staff was me).

3. The board questions the staff.

4. The patron presents his or her appeal of the library director's decision.

5. The board questions the patron.

6. Open the hearing to public testimony. In our case, no one came to speak in support of the patron's concern. But had that happened, our board president would have simply reminded people to keep their testimony to less than three minutes and, in the interests of time, not to restate what had already been said, but say only, "I agree with previous testimony."

7. The board hears public testimony.

8. Close the hearing to public testimony.

9. Staff offers closing statement.

10. Patron offers closing statement.

11. Board member suggests motion. There were several ways this might be handled.

    a. A board member could move to uphold the appeal. At that point, the motion could die for lack of a second, or be seconded and discussed. A positive vote would mean that patron appeal would be granted, and the title would be removed.

    b. A board member could move to uphold the director's decision. Again, the motion could fail for lack of a second, or be seconded and discussed. A positive vote would mean that the title would be retained.

    c. A board member could simply move to keep the title, or not—avoiding the question of who won or lost, and focusing on the issue itself, the disposition of the item.

    d. A board member might move to take some other action, such as re-labeling or recataloging.

12. The board discusses the motion.

13. A roll call vote is called. According to our policies, the decision of the board is final, and no further action is required.

14. Close the public hearing.

At the end, our board president, a humorous and gracious man, did something else that I can recommend. He asked the patron if she felt she had been treated fairly and respectfully and gave the patron full opportunity to respond.

How Our Issue Was Resolved

How did it come out? The patron spoke very well, clearly articulating the value of literacy and the significance of early influence on the formation of lifelong attitudes and behavior.

I spoke about the role of the library: We reflect, not direct, our culture. Parents and children should talk about their values, rather than expecting the library to enforce them for the entire community. While I stated that most librarians share the concern for multicultural, racial, and ethnic sensitivity, we can't police all of our purchases to ensure that this perspective is never contradicted.

My board was magnificent. The trustees were sympathetic to the concern but very aware both of policy and of potential precedent. They had done some of their own research—googling additional information about the authors and poking around to find what else we had by them. They asked intelligent questions and spoke about their own conflicts about messages sent by our society.

In our final remarks, I made another offer. I write a weekly newspaper column. I said that with the patron's permission, I would write my side of the issue, then offer the column to her the following week. I offered to appear with her at various other school committees to talk about children's literature, negative stereotypes, and how to handle them.

The board voted to retain the title, with one dissent. The patron did indeed write a very good column about the issue. She also said that she was impressed both with the process and with the board. While she did not agree with its decision, she believed she had received a fair and thorough hearing, and that given our existing policies, she understood the decision.

In short, the patron could have become an angry enemy of the library. Instead, she is now a friend, a partner in the communication of important issues to our community, and a promoter of significant dialogue.

And that's the goal.

When the Issue Is Bigger Than Your Community

It is important to recognize that for some issues—the use of the Internet, for instance—community or legislative action can continue far beyond the initial local concern and response.

In that case, see the next chapter, entitled "Beyond the Basics." And remember this. Sometimes you cannot stop a social trend by yourself. But you can form allies who will stand with you and speak for you. This means, of course, that you must also stand with and speak for them.

CHAPTER 5

Beyond the Basics: Taking It to the Street

The Pyramid Model

Here is my premise. For a library to succeed, it must not only have a clear grasp of its mission, but it must also secure the support of its constituents. Often, the core constituency—the one that writes the checks—is overlooked. In a municipal library, that may be one person—the immediate supervisor of the head librarian. Or it might be the assistant mayor, the mayor, or the city council.

I am a fervent advocate of the independent library district—one that manages its own money, which it secures by ballot from the community at large. The reason is that in this case the core constituency, the one that determines the library's funding, is the same group that uses the library's services. There is a match between the efficacy of those services and the financial reward.

In some respects, it may be easier to satisfy the supervisor or mayor or council. After all, there are fewer of them than there are people in the whole community. These decision makers can be studied, and strategies can be tailored to win their support. But the odds are very good that those strategies will not be based on the fundamental library mission, but rather on the changing political environment. After all, the library is competing for resources with fire and police departments, roads and bridges, and perhaps even public health. Moreover, there's the peculiar truth that most politicians tend not to be library users, probably because they receive most of their information, by preference, from other people.

The goal of the library district is to secure as much "market share" as possible. There are two reasons for this:

1. A comprehensive analysis of the entire community will result in more targeted, thoughtful, and appropriate services.
2. Libraries that serve a majority of their community well tend to win elections.

How then, should a library go about securing the larger percentage of community understanding and support?

I propose that it should work its way up a "pyramid" of market share.

Market Pyramid

Unreachables?
5% of market

**Answer the Community
Reference Question**
civic club/community visibility
5–15% of audience

Marketing
program/events
surveys/focus groups
community relations
5–15% of audience

Public Relations
publicity
promotion
5–15% of market

Open the Doors
branch operations
circulation, reference, children's, programs, technology
35–50% of market

Opening the Doors

The first step is to open the doors. Libraries have a basic mix of services, including:

- A circulating collection of general adult interest, and staff support both to acquire and to assist the public to find and check out items
- Children's services, including story times, distinct collections, and staff
- A noncirculating reference collection and reference librarians
- Technology in the form of public computers and Internet connections
- Public programs of various kinds (speakers, presentations, etc.)

- Study space
- Meeting rooms

These services—and the policies and processes that govern them—take up the vast majority of librarian time. Libraries are good at all this, by the way. Most of the libraries I visit are clearly well run and well managed.

Moreover, many of the public libraries in the country find plenty to keep them busy. We open the doors, and the public floods in.

Ah, but how much of the public? Based on statistics concerning per capita library card registration, it seems that we can count on about 35 to 50 percent. They find our essential service package very attractive.

But 35 to 50 percent doesn't win elections.

To be sure, many people will support the public library even if they don't use it. This goes back to the credibility of the institution and the linking of "the common good"—whether it be an informed citizenry or the idea of the People's University—with the traditional idea of libraries.

On the other hand, the story of the end of the twentieth century, and at least the first half decade of the twenty-first, has been a growing unraveling of respect for and faith in public institutions. We can't count on public support. Today's Americans think of themselves as consumers to be courted.

Simply opening the library doors, offering our traditional services, is a passive strategy, despite the flurry of activity within those doors. Growing our market share requires something more.

Public Relations

The next step is public relations. This is one-way communication: information about the library distributed to the general public.

What kind of information? Information about the services I just described.

I believe we have two kinds of library users: those who long ago established the habit of library use and kept it, and those who are "captured" as a result of some kind of life change. That life change often revolves around children: pregnancy, parenthood, and homework, for instance. Or it is sparked by another family change: illness or the death of a spouse.

It could also be sparked by work: losing a job and seeking another, or researching some business problem. It might be more generally financial: buying a house or car, or tracking investments.

Or it might be a hobby or home project: Linux, chess, building a deck. Perhaps it's just a simple desire to meet new people by hanging out at a place that doesn't charge admission.

Libraries don't have much control over any of that. Life changes follow their own timetables. But we do know that these moments happen all the time. Yet we will not capture people, even when these opportunities present themselves, unless people know about us.

So the purpose of publicity, of public relations, is to have enough messages floating around outside the library to snag people when they need us. There is another purpose: to tell the library story, to keep informing the public about fundamental library values. One of those values is intellectual freedom.

Whereas most libraries do a good job in the previous stage—opening their doors and providing core services—far fewer libraries do a good job of PR. They don't produce press releases. The flyers and bookmarks they produce are amateurish and inconsistent. The staff fails to build any sort of relationship with local media, resulting in spotty coverage.

Even when libraries do provide a steady stream of information about what's going on in the building, they don't tie that information to that underlying statement of purpose.

But libraries that "get" PR will do better than 35 to 50 percent market share. How much better? I believe they can grow their audience by as much as 5 to 15 percent.

Marketing

The third step is to not just talk to the community through PR, but to ask questions and listen carefully to the answers. This is marketing: two-way communication.

The current generation of librarians has gathered a lot of community data. We conduct focus groups, in-house surveys, and phone polls. Talking to our existing patrons helps us make important decisions: When do enough people have portable MP3 players that we can move from CDs to the new format? And when we talk to people who are not our patrons, we can learn even more.

Primarily, it seems our public still thinks of public libraries as museums of books or perhaps an important introduction to literacy for children. They do not link use to the idea of intellectual freedom.

The best way to understand people is to have frank and probing conversations with them. Ask them about what's important in their lives.

This simple step of surveying the public about a host of issues is the beginning of a community connection. It must be followed up with reworked or new services. It isn't enough just to gather data. The data must be used to drive decisions.

For instance, a demographic shift in a community, away from homes with lots of small children, to empty nests and people moving to retirement, should be reflected in the programs and collections offered at a location. An economic downturn might prompt a surge in programs and materials on resumes and starting your own business.

Marketing means that the public library knows more about the moves of its dance partner—the community—so it's easier to stay in step.

Alas, few libraries get this far, or they survey infrequently, roughly corresponding to the national census. But more conscientious libraries can expect results, perhaps as high as another 5 to 15 percent of market share.

Answering the Community Reference Question

Every day, librarians go through a process known as "the reference interview." People come to or call the library and ask a question. They never, or rarely, ask for what they want the first time. We have to tease it out of them.

Librarians are very good at answering questions. The hard part is figuring out just what the question really is.

This process falls back within the "opening the doors" step of library development. Again, most librarians at the reference or children's desk have honed this skill.

But there are two things that librarians don't do. First, they tend not to track the patterns of the questions—unless a whole class comes in with the same question. Instead, librarians repeat the same interview, and call up the same information, many times. While librarians may, when looking at reviews, say, "I'm getting a lot of questions about Islamic fundamentalism, and here's a book on that topic," the process of aggregating community questions tends to be informal.

The second thing librarians don't do is take their expertise out into the community. They remain trapped behind the reference desk. I've been at many nonlibrary public meetings where a group wrestled with a half-formed question for hours. A good reference librarian could have extracted the question in a matter of minutes. But the nature of the reference interview is one-on-one. It is also the case that groups may have many questions, not just one.

Our society desperately needs reference librarians at its meetings, people with the skill to articulate the information need, and thereby move it closer to fulfillment.

To accomplish this next stage of market building, librarians must leave the building. They must go where the people are meeting.

Of course, sometimes the people are meeting in the library. As I noted earlier, I once joined a group (the Concerned Douglas County Taxpayers) that was very interested in a host of educational issues. Among them were the books at the library. Another of their issues was outcome-based education. Between the first meeting and the next, I was able to dig up enough materials, both for and against, to make a display. When they arrived for the next meeting, I had the display set up in the room and a brief bibliography of articles summarizing the arguments.

At that point, the library (or the librarian) moved in their minds from "the enemy" to something very like a friend.

The credibility of librarians is based on the perception that we are neutral and fair, particularly in providing the information we collect and search.

But there is another lesson we can provide our public. We are not intimidated by questions—in fact, we revel in them! In this way, librarians who are looked at askance the first time they show up at a public meeting are warmly welcomed by the second or third. We make meetings more efficient, and we remove the uncertainty of ignorance.

Such libraries, the ones willing to answer the community reference question, can count on even more market share. Let's say it, too, falls into the 5 to 15 percent range.

The Unreachables

I would like to believe that public libraries could capture 100 percent of the market. But we probably can't. There's a last 5 percent that I call "the Unreachables." These individuals don't have the habit of library use. They don't read the newspaper or track other local media. If they read books, they buy them. They have no immediate use for our databases, or they have identified other sources. They don't talk to their neighbors or attend meetings. They don't respond to library mailings or surveys.

But libraries that connect to their communities keep trying, even when the cause looks hopeless.

Geographic Information Systems

How do you track your "market penetration"? There are a host of traditional library measurements, including circulation per capita, reference questions per capita, program numbers and attendance, and gate count. But I believe that the best measurement is something a little newer that cuts across all kinds of library use: the number of active library cards as a percentage of households within your service area.

In 1996, my library ran an election to increase our mill levy. It was close. The final yes votes just barely reached 51 percent. On the one hand, that's all that's necessary to win in Colorado. On the other, it makes for an intense election night.

After the election, we talked to the people who did geographic information system (GIS) work for the county. We got them to sign a confidential, nondisclosure agreement concerning library patrons, then asked them to match our patron database addresses against the GIS data.

What I was interested in was not just library cards per capita, but households. Why? Because it has been my observation that for many homes, one person brokers library services for the whole family—Mom.

The results of the study gave us various maps, with colors to indicate the percentage of library cards according to various boundaries—cities, developments, etc.

Then we overlapped the precinct results, highlighting the percentage of library cards within each.

Here's what we learned: In those precincts where we had better than 50 percent library card registration by household, we won. Where we had less than 50 percent, we lost.

The stock market has its stock values. The library has library card registration.

Reviewing GIS data annually enables libraries to pinpoint precisely which neighborhoods know about and use their services. This allows librarians to formulate service responses to those neighborhoods. Census data may be available as a layer of data, providing in-depth demographic information. This, in turn, might explain a lot about local use. Library use may decline because a library with a focus on children's services now serves a population that is much older.

Or library card holders may be few because the public library location is not easily visible. With the addresses of households that do not use the library, household-specific mailings are possible.

Again, the philosophy of recruiting as many people in the community as possible has two direct benefits. First, it keeps the library honest about the efficacy of its services, helping it stay actively in touch with the people who pay for it. Second, it ensures that when you do need additional resources, you not only can explain it in terms of your community's needs, you have also secured sufficient credibility to win.

Note, too, that there are many library services for which one often does not need, or use, a library card: browsing, reading magazines, attending meetings, studying.

But the library seeking to gather such data will also seek to integrate its services and promote the use of the card. Meetings held at the library may begin to have targeted displays of materials available for checkout. In-house computer use may require a library card to make a reservation; remote database use needs a card to unlock the resource.

Becoming a Player

Yet if a library intends to do more than simply react to its community, it must take another step.

After all, a library might find itself in a community with a strong social consensus, and that consensus might be in direct contradiction to the core library values of intellectual freedom and privacy. Librarians who find themselves in such a situation face some tough options:

- Give 'em what they want: books that do not challenge or upset the parents of teenage children; children's sections that assiduously avoid any materials on sexuality; Internet workstations that are locked down and patrolled by stern gatekeepers; only music and films with family ratings. This isn't easy, by the way, if only because a G-rated library misses a good deal of the ferment of popular culture. It may be "safe," but it also becomes boring and irrelevant.

It's hard for another reason. Even if a library steers clear of *Daddy's Roommate*, it will still pick up sensitive tales about the death of a grandfather, or the suicide of a neighbor. No matter how timid it may choose to be, a library cannot succeed at the attempt to offend no one.

- Fight. This might be done in a sneaky way, paying tribute to the demands of intellectual freedom while being a little sly about it. Buy *Daddy's Roommate*— but put it in the adult section.

    Or it might be done overtly, with the library making a stand, generating situations that are sure to be divisive. Refuse meeting room access to a religious group because it violates church and state. (It doesn't, by the way, at least, not usually.) Then stage a big brouhaha in the newspapers.

- Move along. Librarians may decide that they have found themselves in a place that doesn't really want a library. Or they believe themselves to be in a trap: trying to provide a service that cannot satisfy consumers because of irreconcilable expectations. Not all of us are seeking a reliable and ongoing source of stress in our lives.

- Become a player. That's the topic of this section. Building on the idea of community connection, libraries and librarians can move from mere analysts and marketers to significant community decision and policy makers.

What Is a Player?

When I conduct workshops on "becoming a player," I often begin by asking, "Who are the players in your community right now?" I quickly write down the names provided on a flip chart.

Then I ask the whole group to validate the list, which eliminates some and may add others, typically those who are indeed powerful in a community, but tend to operate behind the scenes—not the mayor, but the mayor's campaign manager, for example.

What's the point? We know who the players are, even if we are not players ourselves.

How do we know who the players are?

- They are the topics of, or are featured in, news stories. They are the people who are quoted and interviewed.
- They appear at prominent events, often seated at the head table.
- They make decisions that affect the community.

In short, players are visible, and they take action. They effect change.

You don't need a facilitator to work out who the players are. Ask your staff. Ask your board. Interview library patrons. You know them. And if you think about it, you know how they got that way.

Then do what they did.

Show Up

The first step to becoming a player in the community is embarrassingly obvious. You have to show up.

If you believe the greatest threat to the freedom of information will come from your town council, find out where your town council meets. Then attend the meetings.

Or it may be that the real powerhouse in your community is the chamber of commerce. Look up the meeting dates for its board. Consult a calendar of events. Be there.

Are you convinced that the greatest challenges have come from the state house? Get over there for key committee meetings and hearings.

Do you believe that most of the attempts to restrict access to materials have their genesis in the sermons of a local church? Show up early enough to get a seat.

You may have to shop around for a while to figure out who those powerhouses are. But eventually, you'll find out where the recognizable faces congregate.

I mentioned this in "Answering the Community Reference Question" earlier in this chapter. The first time you walk into a meeting, you may be a relative unknown. People will ask why you are there and will be genuinely puzzled to find a librarian in the room.

Your answer should be "This is an important meeting. I want to be a part of it."

There may be so many people that this question may never get asked. You will be an unfamiliar face in the crowd. But the way to become a familiar face is to show up more than once. Don't just show up. Keep showing up.

Your intent is to be recognized. So at some point before, during, or after the meeting, introduce yourself to the people running it. Give them a firm handshake and strong eye contact. Smile. Repeat their names.

I want to take a moment to confront directly a significant hurdle to this fundamental step of political and social action. Some boards may believe that library staff are paid to work *in* the library. This is incorrect. Staff are paid to work *for* the library.

Particularly in those cases where the library is being ignored or constrained, the policy of "don't venture beyond the library doors" will only guarantee the status quo.

Staff members, even directors, may believe that their workload is simply too intense to permit them to leave the building. After all, they reason, if the essential product of the library is a well-managed institution, their first priority must be to ensure that quality.

And of course, this is true. It is important to get your house in order.

But it is also true that many of the essential issues that affect the operation of the library—the availability of public resources or a hostile climate for intellectual freedom—have their beginning outside the library.

If you never leave the library, then you only ensure that you will spend your career responding to the decisions of others.

A strong library presence at community meetings is just as vital—and may be more vital—than internal staff meetings. Make the time, and take the time.

Pay Attention

So now you're at the meeting. People recognized your name and face. Now what?

This is the beginning of the reference interview. Determine, through agenda, minutes, listening, and direct observation, as much as you can about

- the people who participate in decision making. Who makes the transitional statements? Who sums up? Who points out the pitfalls? Who is the peacemaker? What is the pattern of alliances or enmity? Who is approachable?

    How do they talk to each other? That is, what is the style of communication? Is it formal or casual? Direct or indirect? What style of communication is most effective within this group?

- the issues under discussion. What are they talking about? Is there, or is there not, some kind of commonly held set of facts? Librarians have a tremendous advantage here. We can return from a meeting with a list of questions, then quickly research the background.

The structure of a meeting may or may not allow direct participation. But if it does, seek to clarify. Ask questions precisely the way you would at a reference interview. What do these decision makers really want or need to know?

To pay attention means to stay focused, to study, to be in the moment, and to track the trends.

Stay in Touch

There are many librarians who show up, pay attention, and then neglect the most important piece: staying in touch.

There are a host of behaviors that matter here. But staying in touch includes

- passing along information you know will be of interest or use to that person. It's easy to think about someone while you're in a meeting with them. It is much rarer to hear from someone who thought of you when you weren't around.

- "noticing." A person's name can show up in the newspaper because of good news or bad. If that person won an award—send them a note to say you saw it. If the news is bad, send a note of sympathy. Again, it's easy enough to make conversation with people in the normal course of events. What gets you noticed and remembered is your ability to congratulate people for their success and stand by them in their moments of trouble.

I don't think I really understood all this until I built a database of my business contacts. Then I added the various interactions I had with them to the notes field. This made it much easier to see the webs of contact that occur in a community and the many things you may have to talk to people about.

Being a player isn't about power, not really. It's about influence. It's about having enough credibility to be listened to. That means that you remain visible, you remain courteous, and you earn the reputation of being a supplier of reliable information.

The Rubber Chicken Circuit

The obvious example of showing up, paying attention, and staying in touch is working what politicians call "the rubber chicken circuit." Almost every community has civic groups. Organizations such as Rotary, Lions, Civitan, Zonta, the Masons, and others are always looking for programs. They often serve chicken for lunch.

If you only show up when there's a problem, it can be difficult to establish a rapport with a group. Call at least one or twice a year, just to give a library update, or to talk about some new project.

Then, when there is some local intellectual freedom issue, you have already established a relationship with them.

Even better than showing up is active participation. It's harder to lead the charge against the library director when you were picking up highway trash together last week or painting a house for a senior or working a booth together at a festival.

Public Speaking and Writing

This is a small but crucial point. You will be a more effective defender and promoter of intellectual freedom if you are a good speaker. Like most things, that skill depends on study and practice.

I strongly recommend participation in either a group such as Toastmasters, or theater. When I was in my early forties, I tried out for, and got, a role in a community play. That experience, under a good director, taught me a lot about why a "character" (or speaker) is believable.

In essence, it comes down to congruity of action. If your words, your tone, and your body are all sending the same message, you are believable. If you are sending a variety of conflicting messages, you are not believed.

The issue here isn't necessarily about style. Some people are naturally dignified. Others are naturally funny. Some are animated; others are somber. All styles can be effective.

But if you're not comfortable as a speaker, or if you sense that your message is not getting across, get some help.

Public speaking is a skill that improves with practice. All the things that scare you—running out of breath, not projecting well, damp palms, and so on—have solutions. The solution is practice.

Your speaking ability is an asset—or a liability. Effective communication requires clear and consistent coordination. When you're first starting out, it helps tremendously to have an honest and experienced coach.

Using Your Reputation

Now let's go back to a previous scenario: You are a librarian in a place that is heating up around censorship issues.

But now you have three assets:

1. The neutral and common ground of the library
2. A web of community contacts, both among the public and among decision makers
3. Credibility and influence as an individual

Now you can call in a couple of newspaper editors for a public panel discussion on how they have dealt with pressure resulting from unpopular stories.

You can launch a movie discussion program about the boundaries of good taste versus the power of film.

You can host a focus group with local ministers to talk about the role of the library as a neutral information source, highlighting their need for counseling resources.

Behind each of these activities might be more traditional offerings: book displays on the topics of film, film history, discrimination, counseling, media, political censorship, and more. The library might provide bibliographies about other offerings or links to relevant web sites.

Inevitably, some of the people in the group will browse through the materials. Others will want to check them out—thus necessitating a library card.

You can also work to achieve a regular presence in local media—whether newspaper, radio, or cable TV. This gives you the opportunity to get your own viewpoint out to the public.

To quote one of my board members, "If you're not in the game, you're not in the game." There are bound to be goof-ups when you're a player. You will fumble an issue on occasion. You will fight a battle—and lose. But unless you're in the game, you can't win. Nor can you truly be a part of the community and consciously influence the effectiveness of your library within it.

Newspaper Columns

I began writing newspaper columns about the library in 1987. I was the new director (library services administrator, actually) of a municipal public library in Greeley, Colorado.

My board had been very frank with me. Board members felt that many people in the community didn't even know that there was a library. It was far overshadowed by the larger, better-funded county library.

But one of those board members was a columnist for the local newspaper. He set up a meeting with the managing editor and the director of the other library. We pitched the idea of a regular column. At first, the paper thought it was just going to be a "new books at the library" column. But I wanted more than that.

In fact, I wrote a series of essays. They were issued once a week and some of those essays did indeed highlight new materials or programs. But what I was really exploring—as much for me as for the audience—was the question, "What role does the public library play in a community?"

I was also getting into the habit of explaining to people who weren't librarians the reasoning behind library policies and practices. Often I asked for feedback about library policies or procedures under consideration. I have been writing a weekly column (and sometimes more than one) ever since, for a variety of papers.

This discipline has been one of the most powerful strategies I've found not only to clarify my own thinking, but to break out of the cocoon many librarians spin themselves into.

Recently, one of my current board members told me that he learned something from the library that he has tried to apply to all of his other government associations: "Put it all out there. Air your problems and questions as soon, and as publicly, as possible." The newspaper allows us to be transparent, and thereby to earn the trust we require to operate effectively.

I should emphasize that I don't write only about intellectual freedom issues. But I do write about it frequently—a couple of times a year at least (National Banned Books Week is one of them), and some years more than others.

The Format

Before beginning my column, I did some research. I learned several things.

First, the traditional form of a newspaper piece—the main story in the first paragraph, with more and more extraneous details below—hailed all the way back to the age of the telegraph. In the early days, telegraph equipment was unreliable. The gist of the story had to be sent first. This format also allowed editors to cut the end of the story to make it fit.

But that's not how people like to read newspaper stories. They like to hear stories. They want to be entertained. The extraneous details are often the most interesting.

If there happens to be a point to it, all the better. But a piece with a tidy wrap-up is better than one that just stops. Stories need endings.

A casual tone is generally preferred to a formal one. Readers prefer shorter sentences and paragraphs.

I found a DOS software program called "PC-Style" that rated my writing by grade level. I aimed for a seventh-grade level. It was difficult. I was too well educated.

I thought at first that PC-Style was dreadful. Did I have to write dumber, write down to the audience?

But I found that the shorter style didn't limit my scope at all. I could write about any topic. PC-Style forced me to be clear.

Practice helps, by the way. At first, it took me at least an hour to write five hundred to six hundred words. Over time, I learned to crank it out in about twenty minutes.

I also started reading other columnists more critically. The ones I liked best stuck to a consistent structure.

They began with a personal anecdote. This is important. Columnists who endure do so by building a relationship with their audience.

The first couple of times someone may read a column because of the headline. They are interested in the topic. But successful columnists are read not because of what they say, or even how they say it. They are read because of who they are.

Reporters have to be objective and, usually, impersonal. Columnists don't and shouldn't. They should, however, be careful to get their facts right.

Next comes the heart of the story. Most columns have a point, a single argument. Getting smoothly from the anecdote to the argument is what takes practice.

Finally, the end of the column needs to pull the piece together. Columns are most satisfying when they somehow recapture the point with the original anecdote. This is the piece of the format that is easiest to forget and the hardest to achieve.

Because I live in one of the fastest-growing counties in the United States, and because I have lived here now for fifteen years, I find that writing a newspaper column has proved a marvelously effective way to gain visibility and credibility. I've written longer than any elected official has held office. I've outlasted editors and publishers. I've had my picture tossed on the driveways of every house in the county.

I've thereby had the chance to frame a host of debates, putting a "library spin" on topics of the day.

Not every librarian likes, or has the knack for, writing. But the odds are excellent that someone in the library does. The strategy of getting a regular presence in the print media makes sense not only for the reasons above, but also because there is often a strong correlation among people who read the newspaper, people who use the library, and people who vote.

Newspapers are the natural allies of libraries, focusing as they do on people who are literate and curious.

Other Media

But newspapers aren't the only form of media in a community. I know librarians who have very successfully used other methods of getting the word out.

One feisty Colorado rural librarian started a radio show at the local community college. One of just two radio stations within easy reach, it had a solid morning audience. She interviewed local people, raged about various news events, and quickly became known as a lively, funny, passionate radio personality. I was even a guest on her show once, where I learned something important about myself: I cannot and should not speak in public before 9 a.m., although coffee helps.

This librarian managed to be both opinionated and nonoffensive. She might tell someone that she fervently disagreed with their point of view, but then she'd ask what books or movies bolstered that view, and she would secure them for the library. She played fair.

Another librarian, in the Midwest, runs a music program for the local public radio station. His encyclopedic knowledge of all genres makes his show a fascinating, ongoing educational experience.

Here in Douglas County, our local history archivists are regularly featured on cable TV. The county's television crew, DC8 (www.dc8.us)—which has been nominated for and won several Emmys for government TV—works closely with our staff to find and research story ideas. On occasion, they use library settings and actors to bring local history to life.

As a result of that connection, I was asked to be part of an offbeat interview that formed a new program. The cameraman picked me up in his truck, drove around town, and asked me questions. The topic: censorship at the library.

To my surprise, many people saw this show—mainly Gen-Xers and younger. Television reaches an audience that newspapers do not.

On the basis of that program, DC8 began discussions about hosting a book talk series.

The point about participation in media is this. Media is the bully pulpit—an opportunity to frame an agenda, not just react to the agendas of others. Everything you say doesn't have to be about intellectual freedom. But it can be one of your refrains, something that defines your role in the community and builds a base of support.

Politics

Another part of taking the library message to the streets is participating in politics.

But I want to clearly articulate something from the beginning: There is a difference between taking a personal position and making an institutional one. You may be a dedicated Republican, but make sure your library is as accommodating to Democrats. The reputation of the library as a place where all are welcome is a key asset, far more important than who is on top at the moment.

But assuming that you have a policy framework and actual procedures that ensure equal access to the collection and facilities, then why not take it a level deeper?

Some politics is really just part of the job. I know the director of a major urban library. City politics has a profound influence on his budget. When the city council was looking at a significant turnover, he made it his business to show up at all the candidate debates. He attended as many fundraisers as his personal means allowed.

He followed the tenets of "show up, pay attention, and keep in touch." He put a face on the library and reminded all of the potential new council people that there was a library constituency.

When I was the director of a city library, I did everything in my power to make my boss look even smarter than she was. If I saw that an issue was coming up before the council, I got my reference librarians to work up a folder of current citations and clippings. My boss always had in-depth but focused information in front of her, supplied by the library. It's the sort of thing that makes your boss appreciate you.

But I'm talking now about a different kind of politics: the often very hard work that takes place when you are not on the job.

Local

As Tip O'Neill once said, "All politics is local." That's certainly the right place to start. I've worked on a number of local campaigns, both based on issues and on candidates for office. Here's a list of just some of the tasks necessary to a win:

- Fundraising
- Paying bills
- Filing reports with the county clerk
- Writing brochures, position papers, letters to friends and newspapers, press releases, and more
- Creating and maintaining a web site
- Stuffing envelopes

- Distributing and collecting signs
- Hosting local meetings, meet-the-candidate teas, and fundraisers
- Participating in local events such as parades and civic organization meals
- Representing your issue or candidate at official voter information events
- Walking neighborhoods and knocking on doors
- Helping your candidate or executive team take care of personal crises that inevitably come up during a campaign

Until you've done some of this, you truly don't appreciate how exhausting it can be to run for office. It gives you a new respect for all of the candidates, whether they win or lose. Volunteering for a campaign teaches you something else: Winning anything requires a team effort. To put it another way, the battle generally goes to the organized—and librarians know something about that.

It also brings home to you just how important money is. It doesn't take much in terms of personal donations to earn the sincere gratitude of a candidate. A $50 check will do (in 2005). You'd be surprised how few people actually contribute. Campaigning costs a lot of money.

If you think this means that people who donate a lot of money get special attention, though, you are correct. That doesn't mean that your candidate's vote can be bought, or at least, not necessarily. But making significant contributions of time and money does mean that people return your phone calls. You get access and the chance to be heard.

Why put so much time into local politics? There are at least four reasons.

1. Sometimes you know a person of high integrity and insight. You want such people in government. Or, in the case of an issue, you truly believe something should be done to address an important problem. Good citizens put in their time to improve their communities.

2. The connections you make enable you to speak up on behalf of the library. That might be the chance to sway funders. It might be the opportunity to speak up against censorship or the erosion of patron privacy—and get a respectful hearing.

3. The connections you make will directly connect you to a new part of the community. There is a core group of usual suspects who do a lot of the work across all kinds of local efforts. Just listening to the chatter while you stuff envelopes with these people can be an education. The more you know about who does what in the community, and about how things actually get done, the more effectively you can serve that community.

4. The connections may pay off for your own campaign. Sooner or later, every library has to make a request for additional resources. When that time comes, you'll know how campaigns are managed. You will also have invested time in someone else's campaign, which creates an obligation on their part to assist you.

State

Most of what was presented about local politics also applies to state politics. But there are two special kinds of activities worthy of further discussion.

1. Lobbying. Many state library associations sponsor an annual visit with legislators. The legislative agenda for the association may change from time to time. But legislative days typically consist of an introductory presentation about the message, or messages, to be communicated; some brushing up on what your own representatives are up to (legislation they sponsored, key issues of concern); followed by a one-on-one meeting either in their offices or over some kind of meal. Librarians—all librarians—need to participate in these events. Learning to be comfortable talking with people in power is an essential skill. It takes practice.

2. Testifying. At some point in you career, you may be called upon to speak before a state committee about the effects of some bill. You may speak for it or against it. In my experience, here's what works best:

  • Be brief. The best testimony takes less than three minutes, and maybe less than two. But brief doesn't just mean short; it means focused. Your testimony should have no more than two or three main points. Keep it clear and succinct.

  • Be particular and personal. Legislators are looking for real stories. Choose the more powerful funding message: "Libraries help provide important resources to their communities," or "One of our young patrons, a six-year-old boy named Gregor, had a rare form of cancer. Using our Healthline database, we found a description of a new treatment. Gregor is sitting beside me, today, alive, because of his library."

  • Rehearse. When you sit down at a fancy table, in a very formal setting, you can freeze up. Practicing your testimony helps you get through that. You want to look professional and relaxed.

  • Dress up. Most of your legislators are in suits and ties. You'll be taken more seriously if you are, too.

  • Be gracious. Follow the appropriate forms of address.

Remember: Watch what your legislators are up to. When you see something you like, let them know. Very often, people who run for political office are driven by status. Acknowledging their good work is an inexpensive way to let them know that librarians are still out there, and still paying attention.

Federal

Short of direct work on candidate campaigns, federal lobbying for libraries happens in three other ways:

1. Through ALA membership. Join.

2. Through ALA legislative days. Participate, for all the reasons it makes sense at the state level.

3. Through various kinds of national committees. This opportunity may or may not come your way. But when it does, sign up, do your homework, and strive to represent the profession well.

Professional Activity

You are not alone. There are many reasons to be professionally active, but perhaps the most important is the pleasure that comes from talking shop.

I'm making the assumption, of course, that people who work in libraries actually enjoy their jobs. So talking about their jobs is enjoyable, too.

But professional activity does several other things. It allows librarians to maintain perspective, by lifting their heads from the trenches.

It provides networking opportunities—the chance to find people who may have insight into local problems or connections to other opportunities.

Most importantly, professional activity gathers reports of experiments in the field—new programs and services, and how they have been received. It permits the gathering of important trends encouraging or limiting those services.

What kind of professional activity is worth pursuing?

Most obvious is talking with colleagues within your town and city, but not just at your place of work. Call your counterparts at the school or university and invite them to lunch. Look for workshops of mutual interest. You'll find the different views of the same community instructive.

Consider serving on local and regional library organizations, such as system boards. Join the state association and ALA. Run for office, and then learn to delegate.

Don't just attend association workshops; be a presenter yourself. This is not only the best way to learn a topic thoroughly; it is part of a professional responsibility to add to the body of knowledge.

I've come to value most the practice of mentoring.

As a young librarian, find someone who has the skills you would like to acquire. Set up an interview with them. Ask some questions.

Then ask if that person would be willing to mentor you and set some boundaries:

- You are asking for the occasional phone call or e-mail.
- You would like to schedule a regular meeting of some kind—a coffee or lunch just to stay in touch.
- You would like to work together on some project or committee.
- You would like to do some more formal "internship" or shadowing program.

As a more experienced librarian, actively seek connections to your successors. As is the case with presenting, mentoring is an activity that forces you to articulate principles you may not have realized you were applying.

Also, a questioning mind is a wonderful stimulus for exploration. I've worked with young librarians whose questions made me realize that I had no good answer. That prodded me to find a better answer.

I've formally mentored at least three people. One young librarian I actively recruited after seeing her posts on library e-mail lists, corresponding with her there, and talking to her at conferences.

We worked out a schedule: I would call her daily at an agreed-upon time and talk about the day's activities. Once a week, we'd have lunch or coffee.

Then we moved to a weekly phone call and occasional visits.

At about the one-year mark, we met to debrief and decided to present a program on mentoring for a regional conference. This experience allowed both of us to reflect on what we'd learned and bring some closure to that phase of the professional relationship.

Five years later, she moved on to a directorship of her own. It was her dream job, and she was more than ready for it.

And the very first thing she had to deal with was an intellectual freedom challenge—a complaint about a movie.

The mentoring relationship doesn't end. It ripens into friendship and long-standing professional ties. It introduces and reinforces the ideas of collegiality, of turning to each other for support.

Many intellectual freedom challenges succeed and a climate of censorship grows through a sense of personal or institutional isolation. Work within your profession to build a responsive network of allies.

CHAPTER 6

Conclusion: The Fourth Turning?

Kid Stuff

When I began this book, I believed that I had a deep insight into the nature of complaints against libraries. But through my research and thoughts about this topic, I realize that my insight is focused on a time, a moment in history. My own generation has attempted to seize the public library and repurpose it, seeking to make it the enforcer of our growing parental protectiveness.

Many of the challenges my own library has faced have been, literally, "kid stuff." Boomers cannot bear to see the end of our children's innocence. We are the kings who seek to shelter our princes and princesses in a fortress of ignorance. This incipient grief masquerades as heated attacks on our public institutions.

While public libraries will continue to face challenges of the sort I have described, I believe new challenges await us.

Below I profile two cases. I believe them to be harbingers of the next wave of challenges.

I Pledge Allegiance to the Flag . . .

The first case involves an elected official who had an encounter with the Pledge of Allegiance.

Francis Bellamy (1855–1931), a Baptist minister, composed the original draft of the Pledge of Allegiance in 1892. Bellamy was then chairman of a committee of state superintendents of education, and was responsible for a public school's quadricentennial celebration. The Pledge was written to be part of a flag-raising ceremony. Its text ran later that year in the *The Youth's Companion*, a very well-known and popular family magazine.

Bellamy's original version went like this: "I pledge allegiance to my Flag and [to] the Republic for which it stands, one nation, indivisible, with liberty and justice for all." ("To" was added in October 1892.)

In 1923 and 1924, prompted by a group of American Legion and Daughters of the American Revolution representatives, the words "my Flag" were changed to "the Flag of the United States of America." Bellamy protested the change but was ignored.

In 1954, the Knights of Columbus successfully campaigned Congress to add the words "under God" to the Pledge. This had the effect of changing what was a patriotic declaration into a public prayer, in an attempt to differentiate it from something that might be said even in the "godless" Soviet Union. Bellamy left his church in protest of its prejudice against blacks. (He had intended to use the word "equality" in his original pledge, but rescinded it because of anticipated resistance from other superintendents on his committee opposed to equality for women and African Americans.)

Now we come to the story of one Dave Habecker. Habecker was eight years old during the 1954 change in the Pledge, and it had infuriated him. All his life, he had simply kept silent during the words "under God."

By 2005, Habecker had lived in Estes Park, Colorado, for twenty-nine years. He had served on the town council for thirteen years (although not continuously). In general, he was a pro-growth, anti-debt businessman. He was serving out the final year of his term, for which he had run unopposed, when a new councilperson came on board, one Lori Jeffrey-Clark.

Jeffrey-Clark was retired Navy. At her first session, she proposed that the Pledge of Allegiance be adopted at town council meetings. At that time, it was not a part of meetings, nor had it been in the thirteen years Habecker had served. No one else commented on the Jeffrey-Clark proposal, and Habecker remembers saying something like, "It dies for lack of a second."

But at the next council meeting two weeks later, the mayor announced that he was implementing a new tradition: saying of the Pledge of Allegiance before town council meetings. At that time, Habecker made a short speech, saying not much more than that he objected to having to say the phrase "under God," that it was an unconstitutional "religious test," and therefore against the oath he had made to uphold the Constitution. He announced that he would remain silent during it. Then the Pledge was said and Habecker remained seated.

Two weeks later, Jeffrey-Clark came with a couple of surprises. First, set out on the chairs were replica $5 and $10 bills, with the phrase "In God We Trust" highlighted. (Interestingly, that phrase has its own history. It was added in 1863, when a group composed primarily of Baptist ministers argued that the root cause of the Civil War was not slavery, for which they found ample justification in the Bible, but the "godlessness" of our Constitution.)

Second was her nephew's Boy Scout troop. After a short presentation by Jeffrey-Clark, introducing various town officials, she spoke about the display of the flag and flag protocol. Then she remarked, "You may have noticed that Councilman Habecker remained seated during the Pledge." Then she said that although this was his constitutional right, and although she had voted for Habecker, he no longer represented her, and she "wanted her vote back." In a public comment session at the end of this council meeting, her husband, Richard Clark, also retired military, said he, too, "wanted his vote back" and planned to lead a recall effort.

Shortly thereafter, Clark had rounded up some two hundred names and submitted the petition to put it on the ballot. The town announced plans to do so. At this time, Habecker retained an attorney, Bob Tiernan. Tiernan agreed to take the case *pro bono*—up to a point. After that, he suggested, they might speak to the Freedom from Religion Foundation. Later, the foundation did indeed provide some financial assistance.

Tiernan filed a complaint in court, based on three counts. First, Habecker asked that the recount election be enjoined. Second, he asserted that the Pledge itself should be found unconstitutional under article VI, clause 3 of the U.S. Constitution ("... no religious Test shall ever be required as a Qualification to any Office or Public Trust under the United States"). Third, it was a violation of the Constitution of Colorado, article II, section 4, which read in part, "No person shall be denied any civil or political right, privilege or capacity, on account of his opinions concerning religion." (However, the very next phrase continued with the somewhat equivocal, "but the liberty of conscience hereby secured shall not be construed to dispense with oaths or affirmations, excuse acts of licentiousness or justify practices inconsistent with the good order, peace or safety of the state.")

The suit named as defendants the town of Estes Park, the state of Colorado, the federal government, and the three petitioners (Jeffrey-Clark's husband and two others).

Habecker did seek recovery of his expenses, but did not ask for any damages. At the first hearing with a judge, the injunction was granted. Afterward, a Mr. Phillips, author of a recall bill, apparently persuaded the judge that an official may be recalled for any reason or none, hence there was no religious issue. The recall was allowed to proceed.

At about this time, Habecker put up a web site—estespledge.com—in which he listed the petitioners, stated his case, and included several of his responses to letters to the editor. He wrote there, "I will remain seated during the Pledge until every citizen of this country can come to a meeting of this board and not be faced with the choice of respecting their country, their religion, or the will of the majority." He also makes it very clear that he meant no disrespect to anyone or to any religion. He told me in an interview that his daughter is a Jehovah's Witness, who will not pledge allegiance to anything but God. (Habecker is not himself a member of any religious group.) If the purpose of the Pledge was to bring people together, he told me, "it hasn't worked. It is divisive."

He also wrote in a letter published in the *Trail Gazette and Estes Park News* on January 5, 2005, "This recall is a coercive attempt to eliminate dissent. No elected official can ever represent the religious beliefs or national pride of all constituents. These things can only be expressed by the individual."

The turnout was high—the final vote was 903 in favor of the recall and 605 against. That was about one-third higher than the turnout for a subsequent vote concerning whether to grant the town "home rule status"— arguably, a more significant matter. In March 2005, Habecker lost his job.

Since then, both sides have filed for summary judgment, and the matter is being reviewed by the U.S. Attorney General's office.

Catch 22 Patriotism

During my interview with Habecker, I asked him if he thought the apparent community outrage against him had been motivated by patriotism or by religion. While the answer is clearly some fusion of the two— to be patriotic *means* to be religious to some people—he said he thought it had more to do with patriotism. He described a scene in *Catch 22* by Joseph Heller, in which one troop commander hears that another commander makes his men say the Pledge of Allegiance every morning. Not to be outdone, the first commander decides he will make his men say the Pledge *twice.*

"It's like that," said Habecker. "A contest. But you can't quantify patriotism. Am I more patriotic if you have three bumper stickers, and I have six?"

He also described a town council session in which public testimony was taken on the issue of the Pledge. One World War II veteran called Habecker "disgusting," saying that his refusal to say the Pledge was profoundly disrespectful to "the boys who gave their lives."

The next speaker was another World War II vet, a fighter pilot whose plane was shot down over occupied France. The pilot was captured and kept in a prisoner-of-war camp. "I knew we were being liberated," he said, "when I saw the American flag coming over the hill." So understandably, the flag had great significance to him. Nevertheless, "sometimes I don't stand for the Pledge," he said. "It's a private matter; it depends on how I feel. No one here has the right to criticize me," he declared. "And no one here has the right to criticize Habecker."

The Oath He Did Believe In

To an outsider, Habecker did a superb job of clearly articulating the issue. He was careful not to be deliberately offensive. He was also, based on my understanding of the issues, on solid ground. He understood the difference between a patriotic oath and a religious oath. Clearly, he *was* being asked to take a religious oath, and his refusal to do so was enough to cost him his public position.

I also asked Habecker, knowing what he knows now, would he do it again. "Absolutely," he said. "In a heartbeat." I asked him roughly how much the fight had cost. "About $60,000 for this first phase," he said, and perhaps another $60,000 if he appeals. It would take another $40,000 from there to go to the Supreme Court. That puts the cost of a fundamental test of the Constitution at about $200,000.

Habecker also suggested that the government, in the name of patriotism, would try to find ways to dodge, rather than confront, the underlying issue. (He cited *Elk Grove Unified School District v. Newdow*, in which a father objected to his daughter being forced to say "under God" at school. The Supreme Court ultimately refused to hear the case on the basis that the father was noncustodial at the time the complaint was filed, and therefore had no standing.)

"Then why," I asked him, "would you do this again? It cost you a civic position you enjoyed, it set some of your neighbors against you, and it is costing you, potentially, tens of thousands of dollars."

"Because I took an oath I do believe in," he said. "To uphold the Constitution."

Tancredo and Immigration

The second case concerns something Strauss and Howe foresaw way back in 1990. In *Generations* they predicted a growing resistance to, and suspicion about, immigrants. On the face of it, 9/11 would urge some caution. But the current swell of debate focuses more on undocumented Mexicans, hardly a terrorist group.

An example that received brief national attention is the Denver Public Library (DPL). One of the best public libraries in the nation (it won the top spot on the Hennen Annual Public Library Ratings several years in a row), Denver has faced significant revenue loss in recent years. It has also faced some demographic shifts. According to a December 15, 2005, *Library Journal* interview (Berry 2005) with then-director Rick Ashton, "The Denver Public Library serves a large Spanish-speaking population. Denver's population is about 575,000. Thirty-five percent of that public is Hispanic. About 55 percent of the Denver Public School population is Hispanic. Twenty percent of Denver residents speak Spanish at home."

To explore some service models, DPL conducted a series of public focus groups, carefully designed to hit a variety of representative groups. The service models included

- high concentrations of popular materials in a retail-style environment, a "contemporary model"
- the family model, which Ashton describes as "the 1950s with technology"

- a children's library, focused on children from low-income families, often latch-key children

- language and learning libraries, focused on Spanish-speaking adults seeking to learn English, get a GED, or learn basic life skills. It too has a children's component.

Along the way, DPL sought to recruit or encourage staff who spoke Spanish.

In part as a result of some disgruntled or confused staff members, someone passed along a series of distorted concerns to Representative Tom Tancredo (a Republican representing the sixth district of Colorado). He, in turn, wrote a letter to Mayor Hickenlooper of Denver, dated June 21, 2005. This letter was distributed to the media at the same time.

The letter asked a series of questions, more or less a series of "discovery" questions that got almost everything wrong. For example:

1. Was DPL implementing a plan to convert very large sections of several branch libraries—ranging from 10 percent to 62 percent of book and periodical holdings—to Spanish-language holdings? (No such plan existed.)

2. Had the Denver City Council ever debated and approved a plan to convert one or more existing library branches to "Language and Learning" centers with predominantly Spanish-language books, magazines, and materials? (The Denver City Council isn't responsible for library services. That belongs to the Library Commission.)

3. Had the Spanish-language-only concept for branch libraries ever been discussed or evaluated "... as a factor promoting social fragmentation, cultural balkanization and ethnic separatism?" (Again, other than promoting Representative Tancredo's own agenda, there would be little reason to debate a concept that no one had proposed.)

4. Had the library's management announced that only library employees bilingual in Spanish—not Vietnamese, German, Korean, or other languages—would be eligible for raises? If so, is this contrary to civil service rules and blatantly discriminatory on its face? (Library management made no such announcement.)

5. Was DPL assisting "undocumented" (illegal) aliens in purchasing homes through sponsorship of workshops for undocumented aliens in cooperation with the Colorado Housing Assistance Corporation? Does DPL make any distinction between legal and illegal residents in providing its taxpayer-funded services? (With great patience, the mayor responded that, in the first place, "the Denver Public Library does not assist anyone in purchasing homes." In the second place, "the Denver Public Library is not an immigration enforcement agency." This, of course, was precisely what Tancredo's office was suggesting, just as Focus on the Family had done some years before: The public library should assume the promotion of an agenda and a responsibility not its own.)

Shortly thereafter, DPL faced another challenge, the protesting of Spanish *fotonovellas* in the collection. On the surface, the complaint concerned the content of the *fotonovellas*—graphic sex and violence. However, as Ashton himself later said, "The whole episode was just an anti-immigrant, anti-Hispanic gesture in its entirety." It took up a lot of air space on talk radio.

Both issues were resolved. The mayor responded to the list of bizarre questions, and no more was heard. Some *fotonovella* subscriptions were canceled and others were not.

But it is easy to see in these events the faint echo of Des Moines's director Forrest Spaulding beginning the first draft of the Library Bill of Rights in 1938 with, "Now when indications in many parts of the world point to growing intolerance, suppression of free speech, and censorship, affecting the rights of minorities and individuals ..."

There Is *Always* a New, a Next Inquisition

The battle is never over. In my lifetime, I have seen the replacement of one kind of inquisition (a strong social consensus favoring authority over individual values) with another (a divided consensus generally favoring individual rights over institutional tradition or authority). If Strauss and Howe are right, a fourth turning may be imminent, and I may live to see it change again. There is always a new inquisition.

I do see changes in our times, evidence that some Boomers are growing away from self-righteousness and toward a more principled statesmanship. I see aging Gen-Xers who have learned that although most institutions have failed them, some few may be worth supporting. I see rising Millennials, whose collaborative technological savvy brings with it a new internationalism.

Is censorship, then, a thing of the past? Are the guidelines and principles I've tried to explicate here of any use for tomorrow? I hope they are.

For censorship is not dead. It seems so deeply rooted in the human animal that it rises in every age—although most sharply immediately before and after a secular crisis.

I suspect that we are now cycling back to the founding of our nation and will face once more our fears of sedition and of heresy.

Yet I also have confidence in the human spirit, and the twin accomplishments of the First Amendment and the Library Bill of Rights. Public libraries have not always stood for intellectual freedom. But it is the right thing for us to stand for: the untrammeled dignity of individual inquiry and exploration, providing that we do not seek to deprive this right from others.

At the center of our communities, both forum and sanctuary, at the center of our evolution toward free expression and the discovery of truth, remains that shining institution that for me has always been a mark of deep social benevolence: the public library. It is an institution of enduring good, and I am proud to serve it.

APPENDIX

Letters

Samples and Anecdotes

I may as well admit it. Responding to challenges is one of my favorite parts of my job. For one thing, I have the chance to review some (usually) pretty interesting snippets of current culture. For another, complaints often give me insight into my community. For yet another, the process of responding forces me to clarify my own thinking about library responsibilities. Below is a collection of my responses to challenges received by the Douglas County Libraries. I have grouped them by general category. I have also removed patron names, of course.

I have grouped the letters by the age of the intended audience, and then within each age category, by the topics of the challenged works.

By far the greatest number of challenges concern children's materials, and generally speaking, the topic is sex. I present several examples of key issues: *Daddy's Wedding* and *Alfie's Home* present differing viewpoints on homosexuality, and *Mommy Laid an Egg* is a more general work on "where babies come from." I also include a couple of letters on other common concerns.

The next most common age group for complaints is young adult, and again, sex is the big concern. After sex, "drugs and rock and roll" or violence are the hot topics.

Adult materials are occasionally challenged, and again, usually about sex or violence. But the typical tenor of the complaint is "What if a child should find this?"

Finally, I offer four letters about the special case of nonprint formats: Internet access, movies, and music. Frankly, I expected these complaints to be far more numerous. Video and music are more visceral than text. But perhaps they are also more common. Parents who track such things are probably more concerned about TV than about what's at the library.

I have not included letters on all of the potential topics. While I've received a smattering of complaints about virtually all of the areas the Colorado State Library has tracked, these occur rarely. For example, some libraries in other states have reported a surge of concerns about "satanism," typically around the Harry Potter books. But most libraries have responded, reasonably enough, that public libraries are expected to provide best-sellers by mainstream publishers. Harry Potter belongs to a quite respectable branch of fantasy writing. In the U.S., commercial triumph is its own justification.

Children's Materials: Picture Books

A long-standing theme of fairy tales is captured by the phrase "into the woods." Psychologically, this represents the child's departure from the safety of home and the beginning of the exploration of the world beyond. It is also marks the end of innocence and the first encounters with danger. There are wolves in the woods.

But protective parents—and most mid-life Baby Boomers are very protective—want woods without wolves. And they may not want woods at all, unless they are the cute and benign forests of Winnie-the-Pooh. They want Disneyland and Sesame Street. And they rage when they discover that they cannot mandate these fantasies into reality, that their children will still be exposed to a host of threats, both real and imaginary.

The five samples for this category cover the issues that have engendered the most frequent complaints: homosexuality presented positively, homosexuality presented negatively, sex education, violence, and death.

Daddy's Wedding *(Homosexuality)*

August 29, 2000

Dear Patrons (a husband and wife):

Thank you for taking the time to fill out one of our "request for reconsideration" forms on *Daddy's Wedding*, by Michael Wilhoite, as well as attaching your letter.

I addressed the topic of Wilhoite's books in one of my newspaper columns a couple of years ago (it ran June 3, 1998, in the *Highlands Herald* and the *Douglas County News Press*), when someone actually came into the Highlands Ranch Library and ripped the books apart. I made a couple of points in that article that seem to me worth repeating.

First, I bought Wilhoite's first book (*Daddy's Roommate*) at the express request of one of our library patrons. Her husband had left her and their two young sons for another man. She said the book helped her explain the situation to her children. Since then, the book has been checked out many times. I believe it continues to be helpful to some families.

Second, as of today, we have 43,633 books in our Picture Book collection. Out of all these, Wilhoite is one of only two writers who have written books on the subject of homosexuality. His view, clearly, is sympathetic. Another book, *Alfie's Home*, by Richard A. Cohen, takes the approach that although a young child might experience some feelings in the direction of homosexuality, this is a source of confusion that can be corrected through Christian counseling and reconciliation. Here, too, the perspective is biased, but it is likewise based on the recognition that young children have legitimate questions, and literature is one way for parents to deal with them.

As I understand your concern, you believe that materials on homosexuality should not be placed in the general children's area where they are easily accessible. Mrs. Patron, your chief issue seemed to be the difficulty of explaining the fact of homosexuality to your son, a seven-year-old. Mr. Patron, you share that concern, and further state that the book "should not be readily available to the vast majority of children who are not [faced with this situation]."

It happens that I have two children of my own, a daughter, who is now twelve, and a son, who is six. I have shown the book to both of my children as part of my review of it, and I asked them what they thought of it. I find it possible, as I have with other books on controversial topics, to briefly explain to my children what's happening without endorsing the actions of the characters.

Is it appropriate to place books in this area that are anything other than light, entertaining stories? Well, libraries buy what publishers print, thus there are many books in this section on such subjects as the death of a grandparent, mean stepmothers, alcoholism, the loss of a family farm, suicide, and so on. The purpose of these books is not to steal anyone's childhood; but neither is it to protect the child from knowledge.

It might be true that most children don't have to face all of these issues, but it is also true that one purpose of reading is to begin to explore, ideally with loving and thoughtful parents, the complexities of human existence. For example, we also have books about growing up African American, yet some white children find them of interest.

On the other hand, not all books exist for counseling or educational purposes. Some just tell stories. But many good stories often involve things some people are bound to find inappropriate for their children.

Picture books are books designed for kids who have just started to show some interest in reading. Such materials are usually selected and/ or read aloud by parents. Most often, what happens is exactly what happened with you and your son: The parent decides which books come home. Clearly, you both strive to pay attention to what's right for your child, and I commend you for it.

Yet I conclude, as I have concluded after each careful review of the book, that Wilhoite's books really do belong not only in our collection, but in our children's area. Children's books are determined not just by subject, but by style of illustration, size of print, vocabulary, and treatment.

Daddy's Wedding is a kid's book. You may not agree with its message, and that is your right and your privilege. But our collection contains many viewpoints on many subjects about which there is not complete agreement. As you'll see in my attachments, this is precisely what the library is supposed to do.

Finally, as you'll see in our "Reconsideration Process," you have the opportunity to protest my decision to my bosses, the library board of trustees. Their decision is final. The board meets monthly, and all meetings are open to the public. Or, if you have any further comments or questions, please feel free to let me know either in person, by phone, or in writing.

Thank you again for your interest in our collection.

Alfie's Home *(Homosexuality)*

October 23, 1998

Dear Ms. Patron:

Thank you for taking the time to let me know your thoughts on *Alfie's Home*, written by Richard A. Cohen and illustrated by Elizabeth Sherman. As a librarian with two young children of my own, I very much appreciate someone who thinks about what a library has to offer and is willing to share those thoughts with us. It's rarer than you might think.

Please don't be put off by all of the attached documents. As you'll see, our policies require that when someone fills out a complaint form I send them copies of several policies the board feels are relevant. Please review them. It will help you understand the kinds of standards we strive for.

As I understand your concern, you believe that the book is inappropriate for the children's area where you found it. I gather this is because of subject matter, specifically the reference to a young boy being sexually abused by an older family member.

When we decide whether a book should be cataloged in the adult section or the children's section, we don't base our decision only on the subject. We also consider the word choice, the style of illustration, the general tone of the item, and the intended audience. Sometimes, this can be a tough call.

We bought this book to balance another title, *Daddy's Roommate*, which has a generally positive portrayal of a heterosexual boy trying to come to terms with his homosexual father, who moves out and lives with another man. That book is a children's book—far more definitively than is *Alfie's Home*. *Daddy's Roommate* is written from a child's perspective, uses very simple words, has illustrations on par with the illustrations for young children generally, and strives to be both low-key and reassuring. In short, it was much like many of the other books in the children's section that deal with divorce, alcoholism, the death of a loved one, the loss of a farm, and many other topics that children wonder about or read about to try to come to grips with difficult situations in their lives.

Alfie's Home tries to make the point that if a young child is grappling with his own feelings of homosexuality, there may be other causes, that it's not the child's fault, and that a "normal" family life is still possible. In my opinion, I think it just tries to cover too much material over too long a time frame. I don't think it's especially well done, either. Nonetheless, *Alfie's Home* aims to be a kid's book—that's the intended audience, and that's why it is packaged the way it is.

Some have suggested that we put such books somewhere where they are available only by parental request, or in a special "parenting section," which might be in an open area. On the one hand, we'll be adding a children's librarian next year at the Philip S. Miller Library and will be reconfiguring our children's department. I promise to give the idea of a "bibliotherapy" (counseling through books) area some careful consideration.

On the other hand, many of our children and parents find materials only by browsing, by seeing what's in. They don't search the catalog by subject, and they may be too shy or embarrassed to ask a staff member to look it up for them. In my experience, the creation of "special locations"—items segregated from the collection solely because some people find the subject matter controversial—serves only to assure that nobody uses the materials.

At present, I think *Alfie's Home* really does belong where we've put it, although the fit isn't perfect.

As you'll see in our "Reconsideration Process," you have the opportunity to protest my decision to my bosses, the library board of trustees. Their decision is final. If you would like to pursue this, please let me know, or just attend our next regularly scheduled meeting. Or, if you have any further comments or questions, please feel free to let me know either in person, by phone, or in writing.

Thank you again for your commendable interest in our collection.

Mommy Laid an Egg *(Sex Education)*

July 1, 1998

Dear Ms. Patron:

I got another complaint about *Mommy Laid an Egg* back in February 1995. Back then, I read the book and showed it to five moms, two dads, and two kids (with parental permission). I talked about it with all of them and gave some serious thought to the issues both you and the previous person raised about the book.

Attached you'll find a copy of some of our board-approved policies regarding what we add to the collection and why, some basic principles we strive toward, and finally, how we think complaints about library materials should be handled. The purpose of giving you these policies isn't to try to overwhelm you with paper, but to let you know the context in which we try to do our jobs.

We've had the book since August 1993, its year of publication. We used to own four copies. Now we're down to two—books wear out over time, especially well-used ones. The one in Castle Rock has been checked out 78 times. Our copy at the Lone Tree Library (now in storage until the new library opens) has gone out 28 times. That's a total of 106 checkouts, which means that the book has pretty much been out most of the time we've had it—an indication of significant demand and/or popularity.

The opinion of the parents I showed the book to was that by and large, the book was a mostly humorous approach to the subject of where babies come from. (Or as you write, "It describes in a nonthreatening and amusing way how children are made.") Babette Cole, the author, was well known to several of the parents, and admired. However, every one of the parents said that the page showing "some ways mommies and daddies fit together" was either embarrassing or in poor taste.

I asked both of the kids I showed the book to—one (my daughter) had just turned seven, the other was a five-year-old boy—to comment on that page. They pointed to a few of the elements in the picture (clown noses, balloons) and said they were "funny." My daughter said that she thought the pictures of the mommies and daddies were "cute."

I say all this not because I typically take a vote on which individual items should be in the library. The result of such a process would be either intolerable delays in the ordering and processing of books, or the avoidance of certain subjects altogether. Neither is an acceptable solution for an institution that must serve a broad range of constituents in a timely manner. Nonetheless, the introduction of the topic of sex to children is often a touchy area for many parents. I thought I should get some kind of general yardstick of reactions to the book.

Here's my take on the title: I think those two pages in the book were unnecessary. They do border on bad taste. On the other hand, I really don't think that putting the book in the children's section is "irresponsible," as you suggest.

The images of naked people in *Mommy Laid an Egg* are as provocative as potatoes, which they strongly resemble. The drawings are very much like the way children draw—just enough detail to get the point across, but at no time prurient.

Finally, and although I do feel two pages of the book push the boundaries of good taste, I think I should be cautious about yanking books from the public shelf just because a popular and well-established author's sense of propriety doesn't match mine. The book is written for very young children. Because of where it's shelved, children aren't likely to read it themselves; a parent or older person has to pick it out and read it aloud. Given the subtitle of "Where Do Babies Come From?" it seems to me that the topic of the book is clearly identified. While some children might inadvertently stumble across the book, I honestly don't think the exposure is likely to do them much harm.

Based then on the strong evidence of use and the relatively benign and mostly humorous approach to the subject, I have decided to retain the book. Some parents are looking for just such a title and treatment; they have a right to find it here, just as you have the right either to pass it by or to voice your objections to it.

On the other hand, the idea of a "parental shelf" has some merit, too. We'll be working on a modest renovation of the Philip S. Miller Library in the next couple of years. That might be time to address the issue. If we do establish such a section, it would be a good home for *Mommy Laid an Egg*.

As the attached policy describes, you can appeal my decision to the board of trustees, whose decision is final. If you would like to do so, let me know, and I'll schedule you for our next board meeting.

Finally, thanks for caring. If there are a few dubious books in our collection, and there always will be, there are also many other fine titles. I urge you to let us know of anything you would like to see here that we haven't found already.

The public library, like the world in which it finds itself, is something of a mixed bag. It takes all of us together to build a collection that meets the many different needs and desires of our patrons.

The Amazing Bone *(Violence)*

March 28, 2000

Dear Ms. Patron:

I have received your "Patron Request for Reconsideration of Library Materials" form concerning the book *The Amazing Bone* by William Steig. I have just finished reading the book, which I hadn't seen before.

Thank you for taking the time to let me know your concerns. Your comment was, "In light of the currents of the past year (children killing children with guns), we find it unnecessary to make a book available that glorifies violence. This book should be removed from the library."

You are quite right that after such events as the killings at Columbine, violence of any sort has taken on a more personal edge. I think every parent I've talked to has a much greater sensitivity to this issue. I am among them.

Nonetheless, I disagree that the book glorifies violence. The beginning of the book is utterly charming: A young girl (even if she is, literally, a pig) is strolling around after school, taking delight in both the busy productivity of the adult world and the beauty of nature.

Then, as in so many fairy tales, fables, fantasies, and fiction, she encounters something magical: in this case, a bone whose sole gift is that of speech.

The next scene is where the little girl discovers the darker side of life: highwaymen with guns. Suppose I agree with you that the one page where the highwaymen threaten the little girl with a gun is "glorification of violence." Suppose further that I agree anything of this sort should be removed from the library. On that basis, I would also have to pull a great many other classics, among them *The Three Little Pigs* and *Little Red Riding Hood.* The fact is, almost every classic children's story (or, come to think of it, adult story) has some element of danger or darkness. Overcoming the evil is what the story is about. Often these tales are told precisely to prepare our young people to expect that bad things sometimes happen—but then to talk them through the conflict to a positive resolution.

For instance, in *The Amazing Bone,* the highwaymen are scared off by big noises. The fox was not. And although the fox was getting ready to do what a fox probably would do if it could grab hold of a young pig (eat it!), the conflict was resolved without violence—the talking bone dredges up a spell that reduces the fox to the size of a mouse. In other words, by the end of the story no one was shot, nobody even hurt. The little pig got home safely to her home and parents.

You write that you believe the central theme of the book is "violence." I respectfully disagree. I would say the theme is more along the lines of "there is both beauty and danger in the world, and speech can be powerful." You also say there are no positive elements in the book. Again, I disagree. I find much that is positive: the little pig's thoughtful regard of adult activity, her appreciation of a beautiful day, her tender friendship with the magical bone, and her relief at being reunited with her parents.

Finally, I believe *The Amazing Bone* is an altogether appropriate piece of literature for young people—a good story that might cause a shiver or two but ends happily. Kids like a shiver or two, particularly when it's about imaginary danger. I have decided the book should remain on our shelves.

I have attached some of our policies. Please take a look at them. They express what libraries strive, sometimes with difficulty, to achieve.

If you wish to pursue this further, you have the option of referring the matter to my bosses, the board of trustees, whose judgment is final. Just let me know, or feel free to come to any of our public board meetings.

Again, I thank you for caring about what your child reads and what the library offers to the community. Nonetheless, I believe the right response to the problem of violence in the world is not a refusal to discuss it, but the careful attempt to place it in context, lest it catch our children unaware.

I Never Knew Your Name *(Suicide)*

March 27, 1998

Dear Ms. Patron:

When I was a boy, a man who lived down the street from me shot himself. I was about five or six years old.

At the time, I was powerfully curious about what had happened. But none of the adults would talk about it.

A Lutheran minister, who also lived on my street, went over to talk with the surviving wife and their daughters. Later, the minister called some of the neighborhood boys together and asked if we would be willing to help out the family for the summer. (I wound up pulling dandelions and edging the lawn.) One of the other boys asked the minister if it were true that the man had killed himself. The minister said yes, it was true. Someone else asked why. After a long silence, the minister said that he thought the man had forgotten that he wasn't alone. We needed to pay more attention to each other, he said.

The book *I Never Knew Your Name*, by Sherry Garland, reminded me of that lesson. I wish that instead of refusing to talk about the issue, my mother had offered to read me this book.

The library has many children's books about difficult subjects. Some deal with the loss of a family farm, with adult alcoholism, with divorce, with neighborhood crime, with death, and much more. Such books are often written out of experiences much like mine—the child who looked to his or her parents for an explanation and didn't find one.

The young boy in *I Never Knew Your Name* also seemed to be suffering from a lack of attention—in his case, from an absent (divorced?) father. In my opinion, this is one of the most powerful elements of the book. The author not only points out the tragedy of a suicide, but encourages the reader to find in his own loneliness a bridge to compassion for others.

Incidentally, the manager of the Highlands Ranch Library has talked to me about her plans to develop a specific parenting section. This would make it easier for parents to find books that help children deal with their many questions and circumstances. Children do ask for such books, and many parents do look for them as a way to begin to talk about something they know is bothering their children.

I have attached a pile of paper. Our policies require me to send this—not to put you off, but to try to lay out the principles librarians try (sometimes with difficulty) to live up to. I hope you'll look them over.

I believe that *I Never Knew Your Name* is both a good book and an appropriate one for its audience. While I do understand your reservations, please note that the story is told in simple, straightforward language. The large, colorful pictures on each page take care to avoid anything gruesome. What defines an "easy" book like this is precisely these things—language, format, and graphic style—not subject. From classic fairy tales to the most modern fare, children's books have tackled the toughest topics of life, and often handled them more powerfully and sensitively than adult books. They serve an important purpose.

Note, too, that because this book is shelved with our picture books, the children who browse such materials usually need an adult to read them. This gives the adult an opportunity to review the book first.

After careful consideration, I have decided to keep the book in its current classification.

As you'll see in our policies, however, you do have the option to appeal my decision to my bosses, the library board of trustees. Please give me a call if you would like to do that, or to discuss the book further.

Young Adult

The second big life change for our children is adolescence, which kicks off a reaction in the parents. My four examples here concern sex, sex, sex/rock and roll, and death. The concerns mirror adolescent obsessions and parental fears.

Understanding Sexual Identity, Teenage Fathers,
and Teen Pregnancy *(Sex)*

February 16, 1999

Dear Ms. Patron:

I recently received your "Citizen's Request for Reconsideration of Library Materials" concerning the books *Understanding Sexual Identity* by Janice E. Rench, *Teenage Fathers* by Karen Gravelle and Leslie Peterson, and *Teen Pregnancy* by Judy Berlfein.

Attached find copies of some relevant library policies. Don't be put off by all of the paper. This is just my attempt to explain how the library tries to operate and the principles we strive, sometimes with difficulty, to live by.

As I understand it, your complaint is that materials on this subject should not be in the "young children's section." In fact, our children's section runs from preschool age (our "easy" books) up to about twelve years old. It is not uncommon for both our juvenile fiction section and our juvenile nonfiction section to cover subjects for readers through about the age of fourteen.

How do we decide which materials are placed in these sections? There are two criteria: Is the subject of interest to children in this age group and is the presentation of this subject appropriate to this audience?

Of the books you question, I have to say that the subject is indeed of interest to this age group. For one thing, children are able to have children sooner than ever. An article in *Science News* (October 18, 1997) states that "menstrual cycles, which usually started at age eighteen in the 1600s, now start on average at age twelve in the United States." Moreover, while the rate of teen pregnancy is falling, "the teen pregnancy rate in the United States is one of the highest among developed nations and an estimated 78 percent of recent U.S. teen pregnancies are unintended," according to an article in the November 1998 issue of *Pediatrics*. The books on teen pregnancy and teenage fathers are quite blunt about the problems of raising children while you are a teenager. I think information like this is not only of academic interest (children in sixth and seventh grades might reasonably be asked to do reports on the subject), but perhaps of personal significance to young teens.

As for the book on sexual identity, there are many reasons why solid information should be readily available to young teens grappling with the issue of their emergent sexuality. Most compelling to my mind is a 1989 study by the U.S. Department of Health and Human Services. It found that gay and lesbian youth are two to three times more likely to attempt suicide than heterosexual young people. Thirty percent of the completed youth suicides are committed by lesbian and gay youth annually. Information like that presented in *Understanding Sexual Identity* might well save some child's life.

What about the second issue—presentation? A variety of factors go into the placement of a book in the children's section. The most obvious one is length. The next is sentence length and vocabulary. *Understanding Sexual Identity* is fifty-six pages, is divided into very short chapters, and further divided into one or two paragraph answers to various common questions. The other two books have fewer than one hundred pages each, feature lots of pictures, and again tend toward very brief informational sections.

After reviewing these materials, I have concluded that they are correctly placed within our collection. They are on subjects that matter to young teens. They are presented in a way consistent with the education of their target audience. I have decided to keep them right where they are.

As you'll see in our policies, however, you may appeal my decision to my bosses, the library board of trustees. If you would like to do so, or just to discuss the item further, please give me a call, or consider attending one of our public board meetings.

In any case, I do thank you for calling the books to my attention.

Tell Me Everything *(Sex)*

March 30, 1998

Dear Ms. Patron:

I just finished reading *Tell Me Everything* by Carolyn Coman. Your concern about the book was that you didn't feel it was appropriate for the juvenile fiction section, primarily because it refers to rape and menstruation, and contains some vulgar speech.

Attached please find what our policies require me to send when I receive a complaint. Don't let it put you off. These policies just attempt to lay out the principles librarians strive, sometimes with difficulty, to live by.

I wish I could tell you that there is some kind of exact, scientific way to determine precisely where a book of fiction should be placed in our collection. There are several factors, mainly the age and viewpoint of the main character, the length of the book, the general language, and the reputation of the author. But it's not that neat. Some adult works are centered on children, such as *To Kill a Mockingbird*. Some books feature adults, but are for kids—for example, *Doctor Dolittle*. Sometimes well-established children's authors write a book for adults; sometimes the reverse.

Carolyn Coman is a new author, so there's no pattern to build on. Yet the length of the book (156 pages) and the general difficulty of the language puts the target audience somewhere around the end of elementary school, in the high end of our children's fiction. Girls and boys of this age tend to like reading about protagonists just a couple years ahead of them.

Tell Me Everything has some things in common with our young adult novels, which are shelved in a separate area at some of our libraries. The book deals, for instance, with the end of childhood. But most young adult novels also deal in a more pointed way with the issues of late adolescence—a first love, social pressure in high school, increasing responsibilities, and so on. In essence, Roz is a child dealing with the death of her mother, not so much a teenager working her way to adulthood. This, too, leads me to believe that it's probably in the right spot: "bridge" fiction to more complex works, something that challenges elementary readers, but still mostly reflects a child's sensibility.

I've thought a lot about your more specific concerns. It was twice mentioned that Roz, the main character, was conceived when her mother had been raped. While such a circumstance is disturbing, it seems to me that the author didn't dwell on it. It certainly wasn't presented in a detailed or graphic way. Mainly, it established why there was no father in the novel. It may have helped to explain some parts of Roz's close but oddly fearful relationship with her mother.

The subject of menstruation was also mentioned in two places. Again, I did not feel that the topic was dwelt upon. It just established the age of the girl, who was becoming a woman without the benefit of a female role model. My understanding is that this physiological passage is often of great interest to young girls. Incidentally, I recently heard a long radio report about the surprising drop in age of girls reaching menarche. Ten years ago, the average age spread was twelve to fourteen. In 1998, it seems to be ten to twelve. Again, this means that those young girls who use the library at all, look for materials in their own library section that inform them about what they face. (Younger girls wouldn't be reading books of such relative difficulty.) This, too, argues that *Tell Me Everything* is right where it should be.

As for the language, in the 156 pages of the book, I ran across maybe a handful of "cuss words," none too extreme, and most a believable example of a character's speech (usually the uncle's). It happens that my wife and I have a ten-year-old daughter. We don't allow her to use such words at home. But I've noticed that she seems to have solid working definitions of them. Such language is a regrettable but unavoidable part of social interaction. Few children, alas, would encounter such words in this book for the first time.

On a more personal note, my sole surviving parent died last October. I found Roz's quest to understand what happened to her mother, and why, particularly poignant. To be honest, it left me in tears. A man can be in his forties and discover that, in some ways, a child still lives inside him. Maybe that's good news.

Tell Me Everything is a sometimes elusive, but well-written and powerful book. The real tragedy is that very few people will find it. We tend to lose a lot of readers as they move from childhood to the teen years. If they could get their hands on books like this one, they might understand in a more direct way the power of literature to illuminate their lives, to make sense of the feelings that—too often at that young age—threaten to overwhelm them.

In sum, I really do think we got this one right. It belongs in the children's fiction section, often the most overlooked section the library has.

If you disagree with my decision to keep the book where it is, either give me a call and we'll talk about it further, or I'd be happy to let you speak to my bosses, the library board of trustees. In the meantime, thanks for caring about the books we offer. That concern is rarer than you might think.

Forgotten Fire *(Violence)*

April 20, 2001

Dear Ms. Patron:

You gave a "Pen Your Thoughts" note to the manager of the Highlands Ranch Library back on March 13, about the book *Forgotten Fire*, by Adam Bagdasarian. You said you requested that we purchase the book, which we did, that you read it, and that you found it "an interesting tale of the Armenian Holocaust."

However, you also expressed concern about our having cataloged it in the young adult (YA) area. You wrote that "this story has great value in knowing past history but may not be appropriate for a young viewer/reader." Therefore, you requested that we re-catalog the book as adult fiction.

The manager passed this along to me because she knows what great interest I take in patron comments about our holdings. Since receiving the book, I've not only managed to get it read (finally!) but also to have my thirteen-year-old daughter, Maddy, read it. We've been talking about it for a couple of days, and I wanted to let you know my take on the book.

First, what an awful story. Since my early childhood, I've known a lot of Armenians, but never knew, or forgot, why they had such a hatred of Turks. Now I know. *Forgotten Fire* captures a powerful "immigrant story." As you say, the story does indeed have great value. The quote from Hitler at the beginning of the book ("Who does now remember the Armenians?") does much to explain why the book was written. We must remember such stories.

Second, I paid a lot of attention to the manner and the format in which the story was told. Generally speaking, the language is simple and straightforward. The protagonist of the story, Vahan, is twelve years old at the beginning of the book; fifteen, at the end. The story focuses not on the larger political events, but instead on the specific events in the life of this boy. The book is approximately 270 pages long.

All of that tends to add up to a "YA" novel—a personal tale involving a wrenching, life-altering transition in the life of a teenager. On the basis of word choice, format, and character, *Forgotten Fire* fits pretty comfortably alongside our other YA materials. My daughter agrees. When doing an Amazon.com search, I find that it has been identified as one of "the best young adult books" by several readers.

But third, I think your real issue is appropriateness of content. I've given a lot of thought to that. I share with most parents the deep desire to shelter my children, to protect them from the many horrors of life. Some of those horrors will no doubt find their way past all of my defenses. But does an adolescent—between the ages of twelve and seventeen, generally—really need to be exposed to a story in which a ten-year-old girl is raped to death, or a thirteen-year-old boy has to stand by and watch his brothers shot or see his sister die of poison?

I can certainly understand someone taking the position that no, children do not need to be exposed to this. We might agree that there is far too much senseless violence in the media as it is.

On the other hand, this is different in two ways from the all-too-common, casual street violence of television and film. First, it's print. The images in the book are not gratuitous close-ups that burn straight into your eyes and mind. They are descriptions. They run through a linguistic filter. They have a literary context.

Second, and tragic though it may be, the story is true. Such things, in fact, happened to ten-year-old, twelve-year-old, and fourteen-year-old children.

I sincerely hope that my daughter never has to go through anything like this. But in the midst of war, in the midst of ethnic conflict, even in our own suburban schools, such things happen. Is it better for our young adults to think history is remote, distant, detached from life, safe? Or is it better for them to understand the true human dimension of history, and the depths to which human beings may sometimes sink?

As I talked with my daughter, I realized something else. We don't clearly remember everything we read. But books, nonetheless, constitute a kind of distilled experience. Vahan's story was once the private property of a family, shared from uncle to child. Now it becomes a part of my memory and a part of my thirteen-year-old daughter's.

I believe that should she ever find herself in an analogous situation, she will not be quite as bewildered, as helpless, as she might have been otherwise. In some part of her mind, she will understand, and perhaps be able to act, when otherwise she would be a victim.

It is this belief in the power of literature to help us understand life, to prepare us for situations we may never encounter, that is part of the reason I became a librarian. I believe that if such things as described in *Forgotten Fire* can happen to adolescents, then adolescents must have the freedom to read about them, for their own safety.

The part that haunts me about the book is that so much depended on luck. Some children are murdered. Some live. Sometimes, survival is solely a matter of chance. It's one of life's hardest lessons. It is, as many parents have discovered when talking about Columbine with their children this week, very difficult to explain just how unfair life—and death—can be. But the alternative is silence and happy talk. Sometimes, about some things, children need to know the truth.

At any rate, I've decided to keep the book in the YA section. But I've also directed our technical services department to buy some extra copies, some of which we'll put in the adult section. You found a good book for us, and I hope it will find the audience it deserves, whatever the age of the reader.

Thank you for your thoughts, and please feel free to contact me if you would like to explore this further.

The Long Hard Road out of Hell *(Sex, Drugs, and Rock and Roll)*

March 16, 1999

Dear Ms. Patron:

Well, I finally got through *The Long Hard Road out of Hell*, the biography of Marilyn Manson. As I expected, it was difficult to read it straight through. Sorry for the delay.

At first, I decided that Manson was pathologically disturbed, deranged by bad genes and a peculiar upbringing. Then I reconsidered: He was pretty shrewd, a very young man who put over a huge con on the American public and got wealthy in the process. Then, after reviewing some of the clippings he included about opposition to his tours, I thought Manson provided a fascinating commentary on the social and cultural climate of America. Then I thought that he was a remarkably self-deluded individual who did a good, if unintentional, job of showing what a waste of time it is being a shock rocker. What's the message supposed to be, anyhow? Become a satanist, take drugs, have indiscriminate sex, and you too can wake up in a hospital? Having finished the whole book, I honestly don't know what to think.

The book was reviewed, mostly positively, by a variety of magazines, including *Rolling Stone* and *Village Voice*. I liked this line from a frankly negative review by *Entertainment Weekly*: "Of course, some people will pick up *Hell* for its tales of backstage debauchery. They might be disappointed: Despite scene after scene of drug-addled depravity, what's really shocking about Manson's rock and roll lifestyle is how boring it is to read about."

There are several things that do seem clear about the book. First, for reasons beyond my comprehension, Manson has many thousands of fans. *Rolling Stone* refers to him as an "icon of popular culture." Manson is a media creation, like so many of the people other people want to read about. But he is a "success."

Second, HarperCollins, meanwhile, is a long-standing mainstream publisher. It's not a publisher of pornography, although I'll admit that the line is pretty shaky sometimes. Libraries often buy celebrity biographies, and we certainly buy many titles from HarperCollins.

In short, the reason the book is in print at all is because the book-buying public is willing to pay for deliberately outrageous stories. Many people pick up celebrity biographies for precisely this kind of titillating exposé. While not a particularly attractive truth about humanity, it does explain both why such a book is published (because it sells), and why you find it in libraries (our patrons most frequently request books that tend to sell well, and we tend to buy what our patrons ask for).

As our policies mentioned (previously enclosed), the library doesn't endorse every book we buy. We simply reflect our culture, which includes excesses at both ends of the moral and political spectrum. While Marilyn Manson is, to my way of thinking, hardly a role model, he is nonetheless a mainstream "star."

I understand your main concern to be that you didn't think this should be available for children. This, of course, is precisely why we put the book in the adult section of the library. But it is also true that we don't make any special effort to stop children from checking out materials from anywhere in the library. On the other hand, a thirteen-year-old isn't exactly a child. He is a teenager, a young adult, thus at an age when young people tend to start exploring some of the more risqué sides of human behavior. He's old enough to follow the story, whereas a young person wouldn't even try.

One of the underlying premises of public librarianship is that individuals, not government employees, should decide what they want to read from library offerings. It is also a premise that parents, not public librarians, should be the ones to set limits on what their children—and only their children—may or may not read. But I also gather that your son disobeyed you—that you told him not to read the book, yet he did. I continue to be impressed that you paid attention to what your son was reading, and even got him to summarize the book for you. This strikes me as the healthiest response: Talk to your child about the things that clearly interest him enough to investigate them. And I'm sure this is difficult.

The sad truth is that such goings-on as recounted in *The Long Road out of Hell* do exist. But I also think that some young people are drawn to this in much the same way as perfectly upstanding adult citizens enjoy reading the occasional murder mystery. Reading about something isn't the same thing as doing it, and in fact, may point out the consequences of behavior and convince the reader that such a course isn't worth pursuing.

At any rate, after careful consideration, I have reluctantly concluded that the book, despite its disagreeableness, has a place on public library shelves, if only as a cautionary tale. I've decided to keep it. As mentioned in the policies I sent you, you do have the option of appealing this decision to my bosses, the library board of trustees. If you want to do that, let me know. Meanwhile, do keep talking to your son. He's lucky to have you.

Adult Print

Almost everybody thinks about, and is motivated at some level by, sex. It does seem that in the United States we are particularly obsessed with it, perhaps as a result of our Puritan founding. It's a potent formula: Forbid, then advertise.

For advertise we do, in the relentless flood of music, still images, film, and print. Sex sells. The three examples below focus on the presence of true erotica in our collections. Sometimes such complaints are couched in language that suggests the real concern is "protecting the children." But I think the core issue is the deep fascination and revulsion our culture promulgates about our sexuality.

The Delta Ladies *(Sex)*

June 16, 1997

Dear Ms. Patron:

Thanks for taking the time to fill out a "Citizen's Request for Reconsideration of Library Materials" form. As you'll see, that action requires me to respond in several ways. One of them is to send you our various library policies, which you'll find enclosed. Another is that I must examine the item myself and let you know what I've decided to do about it.

About the policies: Don't be put off by all the paper. These are the things librarians try to live up to, the principles we strive to uphold. At times, it can be a challenge.

I read *The Delta Ladies* over the weekend, and it was eye-opening. I also did a little research on "Fern Michaels," a pseudonym of two ladies, Roberta Anderson and Mary Kuczkir. Both were self-described housewives who wrote an historical novel on a lark. To their surprise, it became a best-seller. Since then, they have become quite popular, and in fact, among the most successful writers in the market. To quote from a reference work called *Contemporary Authors* (volume 115), "Anderson attributes much of her success with Kuczkir to their ability to portray sex as romantic instead of pornographic. 'We get letters from reader[s] all the time thanking us for making sex pretty ... that's half the formula in a nutshell. The whole formula is violence and pretty sex.'"

Here's my personal reaction to the book: Most of the characters in this book have the morals of monkeys, and I can't help but wonder if I'm slandering monkeys. The scenes you cite—the sister slipping into bed with her brother, the attempted murder, the passivity of the mother at the end of the book (and the abandonment of the daughter by the father)—are indeed the worst of the lot.

On the other hand, it was pretty clear that the authors thought so, too. The one sex scene that was not described at all was the sister sleeping with her brother. Afterward, the brother was horrified and shamed by what he had done. The father, mother, and Cade Harris all roundly condemned the incest. In the fictional world of Hayden, Louisiana, wholesale adultery and prostitution are perfectly acceptable, but incest is over the line. Why nobody did anything to help the clearly disturbed daughter is beyond me.

But despite my feelings about the book, our two copies of the paperback have together circulated some fifty-eight times. We even have a copy in large print, which has been checked out nine times. Most readers of Fern Michaels seem to have a good idea what they're getting and enjoy the books enough to propel the authors into the ranks of best-sellers and ensure their financial success.

In short, although *The Delta Ladies* isn't my cup of tea, many readers have enjoyed it. Sex, violence, and mental illness have long appeared in literature and popular fiction, from Shakespeare to modern romance novels. Some books handle these topics more tastefully than others.

As I hope our policies make clear, the library doesn't necessarily endorse the views expressed in our materials. Yet the public can reasonably expect us to carry the mass-market writings of popular authors, however much they might shock or offend some of our patrons. After weighing all this, I have decided to retain *The Delta Ladies* in our collection.

Also in our policies, you'll see that you have the right to appeal this decision to the library board of trustees. These are my bosses. If you would like to do that, let me know, and I'll schedule you to appear before them.

Otherwise, feel free to give me a call, write me, or stop by to discuss this further. And thank you again for caring about what you find in your library.

Captivated *(Erotic Short Stories)*

March 19, 2000

Dear Ms. Patron:

I am responding to your "Patron Request for Reconsideration of Library Materials" regarding the book *Captivated,* a collection of short stories by Bertrice Small, Susan Johnson, Thea Devine, and Robin Schone.

Under our policies (attached), you'll see that I have to read the book before I can respond with a decision. Life has been hectic lately, and it took me weeks longer to get to this than I had hoped. My apologies for taking so long.

But I have read and thought about the book, and I have looked at a number of reviews published by book critics and "romance" fans.

Your primary concern is that the book is labeled as romance, but you believe it is sufficiently different from most of our romance titles—mainly given the themes in the first story of very explicit sexual encounters and issues of sexual domination—that it should be at least relabeled.

I have to confess that I'm not a big romance reader. But it's clear that *Captivated* does indeed contain far more graphic language and situations than the usual Harlequin. But I was surprised to discover that one of the authors, Thea Devine, writes for something called the Harlequin Temptation series—a subgenre of romance stories that are most properly cataloged as "erotic fiction," but do appear under the Harlequin label. Bertrice Small has won a host of awards, among them Historical Romance Novelist of the Year (1983), Best Historical Series Author Award (1986), and Career Achievement Historical Fantasy Award (1991). While I haven't found much else by or about the other two writers, it seems clear (based on Amazon.com reviews) that for some readers, erotic fiction of this sort is romance, albeit a little on the fringe.

It seems to me that there are two ways to look at this. You mention that you've been reading romance novels for twenty-five years, so you know better than I do what the general norms of the genre are. On the other hand, sex does play a significant role in most actual romances. While in *Captivated* the sexual scenes are outlandishly extravagant, that's true of most other things in romances, too, particularly the historical romances I've read. The women are more beautiful, the men more handsome and roguish, the situations altogether gothic. That's why people read fiction in the first place: In some ways, it's better than life.

I noticed that in all of the stories in *Captivated,* the ending was "happy." There was a lot of sex, but the point of it all was love, an enduring if steamy relationship.

You mentioned that the blue label appears on the book, as indeed it does. Yet there are other indications on the book itself that this isn't the typical Barbara Cartland book. The subtitle is "Tales of Erotic Romance." On the back of the book, each of the stories is described in language that should give most readers a good idea what to expect: "lascivious games," "seduction," "the pleasures of the flesh," and "sensual surprises."

Most of our romance paperbacks don't have subject headings. But I notice that we have more than 2,200 "romance fiction" titles in our catalog, another 1,300 "historical fiction," and just 47 "erotic fiction." All of this tends to reinforce your point, I think, that erotic fiction doesn't fit the usual definition of romance.

I think we do need to go back and change the catalog entry for *Captivated.* It is not listed as "erotic fiction," and it should be.

However, based on what I read on Amazon.com, I think it really does fall within the overall readership of romances. All of the authors in the book have achieved some popularity, as judged by sales. On the other hand, I notice that this particular book hasn't been checked out very often—our four copies have gone out just thirty-one times. Based on that record, I doubt we'll be greatly expanding this kind of offering.

Ms. Patron, you asked why we bought such a book at all. I think the best answer is that the job of the library is to reflect the offerings of publishers and to respond to public requests for such material. We do strive, of course, for intelligent representation, as well as for a core of authoritative reference works. The growing popularity of this new subgenre of romance novels nationwide may not lead us to have a high opinion of today's publishing climate. Yet many perfectly respectable and law-abiding citizens find such works a rollicking good read.

Please review the attachments—an attempt to summarize the principles public libraries try, sometimes with difficulty, to live by. If you would like to follow up with me, or take the issue to my bosses, the board of trustees, just let me know.

Meanwhile, thanks for letting me know your frank opinion of this slice of our collection.

Certain Prey *(Violence)*

March 6, 2000

Dear Mr. Patron:

I am responding to your "Patron Request for Reconsideration on Library Materials" regarding the book *Certain Prey* by John Sandford.

Under our policies (attached), you'll see that I have to read the book before I can respond with a decision. Library directors, like the cobbler's children who go without shoes, seem to have little time to read. My apologies for taking so long.

But I have read and thought about the book, and I have looked at a number of reviews published by book critics and mystery fans.

Your complaint, as stated, is the "language, vicious murders throughout. Just plain trash!" You found nothing positive in the book, and no age for which you would consider it appropriate.

It's hard to argue about the language and vicious murders. The book is, after all, about a Mafia hit woman and a rapacious female lawyer who happens to be a sociopath. The language reflects the background of the characters: cops and murderers.

I have to say that I am not a regular mystery reader. This was the first Sandford book I've read. I understand, however, that *Certain Prey* is the tenth in a very successful series of books he has written featuring "prey." The detective in the series, Minneapolis Deputy Police Chief Lucas Davenport, has many fervent admirers among murder-mystery readers. I spent some time looking at comments on Amazon.com and find that in general, fans found *Certain Prey* a worthy contribution to the series.

We own several versions of the book: hardback, large print, and cassette. Together, these copies have been checked out by our patrons more than three hundred times. Moreover, we own some twelve other titles by Sandford, and they all move fairly briskly as well.

Popularity, of course, says nothing at all about an item's quality, as demonstrated by the recent TV debacle involving the woman who married a millionaire. But it seems clear to me that Sandford is a well-established writer whose books have a dedicated following. Many of our patrons are ardent mystery fans. His works have found appreciative readers in Douglas County.

Now for my personal reaction to the book. I thought the lady lawyer character was both repulsive and unbelievable. The book struck me as hanging altogether too much on unlikely coincidence. On the other hand, I thought the detective was a sympathetic character. So was, I'm a little baffled to admit, the Mafia hit woman—a sort of Horatio Alger character, if you don't get too picky about her choice of profession. In sum, I suspect my own judgment of the book is closer to yours than to that of the mystery aficionado.

Nonetheless, I've decided that we should keep the book, mostly because I can't think of any solid justification for the public library to refuse to carry the works of well-established and popular mainstream authors. The job of the library is to reflect the offerings of publishers, and to respond to public requests for such material. We do strive, of course, for intelligent representation, as well as for a core of authoritative reference works.

Sandford's popularity may not lead us to have a high opinion of today's publishing climate. Yet many perfectly respectable and law-abiding citizens find his works a rollicking good read. That's what makes this job so interesting—seeing the sometimes utterly inexplicable patterns of public taste.

Please review the attachments—an attempt to summarize the principles public libraries try, sometimes with difficulty, to live by. If you'd like to follow up with me, or take the issue to my bosses, the board of trustees, just let me know.

Meanwhile, thanks for letting me know your frank opinion of this slice of our collection.

Media

For all of the hubbub at the state and federal levels about this, I find that complaints about the Internet and music are the least frequent. I have had only four complaints about the Internet. I have had only one complaint about a music CD. Complaints about movies seem to be picking up.

My favorite story about Internet use occurred at a neighboring library district. A staff member stepped out of the staff room and saw two people sitting at Internet stations. One was a fifteen-year-old boy. The other was a middle-aged woman. The fifteen-year-old boy was looking at graphic sexual images. The staff member, taken utterly by surprise, screamed. (That's not the actual policy for staff responses. But it's not bad.)

Then the middle-aged woman looked at the screen. She screamed, too. Then the middle-aged woman turned to the staff member and said, "How dare you let my son look at that in the library!"

Internet Access by a Minor

This complaint came via email on December 12, 2002, from a local pastor. He wrote:

> I am a children's Pastor for a local church. I was recently confronted by an eleven-year-old girl whom I pastor, regarding searching the Internet at the library on University and Highlands Ranch Parkway. She had typed in a search parameter of "hologram" for a school project, and graphic pornography immediately show up on the screen.
>
> Are there any restrictions on the Internet service that you have in the library? If so, then I need to find out how she got into the pornographic Internet mess. I cannot stress enough how much this disturbed her. Eleven years old! This happened five days ago, and she was a mess! She was too disturbed to tell her parents, and I want to know what to tell them about OUR public library. Thank you for your time in answering my questions.

My response, also via email:

First, I offer my apologies for anything that may have disturbed your young friend. Second, I'd also like to give a little background information. I've just tried that same search, and I could not replicate the results. Your young friend may, however, have used a different search engine. I still don't think things would happen quite as you may have had them described to you.

In general, typing ANY search term into a search screen will not cause a graphic to "immediately show up on the screen." (Typing it as an

Internet address might—but I couldn't get that to happen, either.) She would get a summary list of sites. Usually, those sites would be described in a paragraph after the Internet address. Thus, most people would have a good idea what they were selecting.

Third, I've given a couple of hundred hours to the study of this issue and have reluctantly concluded that the Internet—a worldwide, unregulated telecommunications network—is a bigger thing than a local librarian can truly control. As you'll see below, we're making a valiant effort. But as with so much else in society, it still takes alert parents and honest children.

Fourth, our library board of trustees has adopted a policy entitled, "Access by Minors to Internet Resources." It reads as follows:

The primary mission of the Douglas Public Library District is to provide public information. Nevertheless, it is the intent of the Douglas County Libraries to limit access by minors to Internet resources that are obscene or illegal.

We do this in a variety of ways:

We have created web pages (see our Kid's Corner at douglas.lib.co.us/kids_corner/ and Teen Scene at douglas.lib.co.us/teen_scene/ designed to direct minors to positive, high-quality sites, created or reviewed by librarians.

We offer various classes that teach parents and children how to search the World Wide Web safely and effectively. See douglas.lib.co.us/about_us/programs/netclass.htm.

We provide supervision of public space. Minors, like adults, are expected to behave in a civil and appropriate manner in the library. The display of visual material that is sexual in nature or that might be considered immediately offensive to others, constitutes rude behavior in many circumstances. In such circumstances, at the discretion of library staff, patrons will be asked to cease such behavior. If they do not, they may be ejected from the library, and risk the loss of future library privileges.

We also supervise public space by placing Internet workstations, wherever possible, in direct line of sight of our staff. Further, we will investigate all complaints lodged by other patrons.

We will limit access on Internet workstations in the children's area in one or several ways: We may supervise their use through observation, or the workstations may be filtered, run through proxy servers, or be placed in "kiosk" mode, at the director's discretion. If filtering software is used, it will be so identified on the terminal. Blocked pages will point to a library-sponsored web page that permits the blocked site to be challenged or reconsidered. Technology, and various technological tools, are changing rapidly. Library staff shall seek to remain current concerning various options, and may experiment with them from time to time to better understand them. It is understood that no technology has proved to be 100 percent effective in allowing only "good" content and blocking only "bad." [Note: Our Internet terminals in the Highlands Ranch Library's children's area do, in fact, use filters.]

We will not filter terminals outside the children's area. Parents, may, however, direct that their minor children use only filtered terminals.

The library considers this decision to be between the parent and the child and it is up to the parent to enforce it.

The library reserves the right to monitor Web sessions in order to ensure system security. These sessions may be reviewed anonymously and remotely by library staff. All transactions will be considered confidential, except in those cases where illegal activity is observed, in which case Internet connections may be terminated, and information may be made available to the police in accordance with the provisions of C.R.S. 24-90-119.

Enforcement and consequences. No one, minor or adult, has the right to use public property to commit crimes. At the same time, no policy can ensure that crimes will never be committed. If minors are found to be accessing materials that may be, at the discretion of library staff, obscene or illegal, the minors will be ejected from the library, and may be barred from future use of library resources.

Adopted by the Board of Trustees, Douglas Public Library District

Leaving Las Vegas *(Video, Sex)*

April 18, 2000

Dear Ms. Patron:

Thank you for submitting a "Patron Request for Reconsideration of Library Materials" form regarding the movie *Leaving Las Vegas*. Your concern, as stated on the form, is that the item contains "Sex, filth—not for children."

It is certainly the case that the content of the movie is adult in nature. A man goes to Las Vegas to drink himself to death, and there he forms a relationship with a prostitute who faces daily threats—and more than threats—of violent abuse. I agree with you that such a movie is "not for children." This is why we shelve it with our other adult videos. The video case is clearly marked as an "R" movie. The back cover clearly states the content. To my knowledge, no child has ever sought to check it out, nor can I imagine that one would. Moreover, I would trust that no parents would allow their children to watch it.

Why does the library own it at all? Well, as you'll see in the various attachments, the Douglas County Libraries has adopted some fairly specific guidelines for the purchase of adult feature films. First, we select them from titles suggested by the National Endowment for the Arts, the American Film Institute, the Library of Congress National Film Registry, the Academy of Motion Picture Arts and Sciences (Academy Award winners in all categories), Hallmark Hall of Fame, PBS, and the BBC.

Leaving Las Vegas won the 1995 Best Actor Oscar for Nicolas Cage and got a Best Actress nomination for Elizabeth Shue. It was also nominated for Best Director and Best Screenplay. As noted on the back cover of the video, "this emotionally charged powerhouse of a film graced over 100 '10 Best Lists'—including Roger Ebert's #1 Movie of the Year."

In short, although the content is not only "not for children," but not to the taste of many adults, it has been recognized as a fine film, one of the best on several levels, by numerous sources. We bought it because it fits our profile for purchase. That doesn't mean, necessarily, that we endorse the movie. It does mean that we believe such award winners are appropriately housed in the library.

I have also attached several other policies about how and why the library buys various materials. I understand that this item, and no doubt many others in the library, will shock and offend some of our patrons. Nevertheless, it is the mission of the public library to reflect some representative sample of the culture around us.

I don't have precise figures on just how many of our movies fall into the category of "shocking and offensive." It's not only "beauty" that's in the eye of the beholder. But by far these selections are in the minority. Most of our video collection consists of nonfiction titles (science and nature films, biographies, how-tos) and children's movies.

But some of our choices do, and probably always will, upset some of our patrons. That's because, as I see it, there are things in the world around us that are equally upsetting. Sometimes writers and moviemakers focus on those things. They become a part of our culture, good or bad.

So although I share some of your misgivings about this movie, I do believe it belongs here, just where we put it.

If, after reviewing the various attachments to this letter, you'd like to discuss this further, please give me a call. Or, as you'll see in our policies, you do have the option of appealing to my bosses, the library board of trustees.

Meanwhile, thank you for sharing your frank opinion of the merits— or lack thereof—of *Leaving Las Vegas*.

Please call me if you have any further questions or comments.

Absolute Power *(Video, Sex and Violence)*

April 10, 2002

Dear Dr. Patron (a woman):

Thank you for sharing your concerns about the video *Absolute Power*. It took me a while to carve out the time to take this home and watch it, but I managed to do that last night.

As you put it, your concern about the video has three parts: first, you objected to "the graphic, brutal rape and murder at the beginning" (after which you no longer watched the video); second, you were "concerned that children are able to check this material out without adult supervision"; and third, that "there is no warning on the box concerning the violent, sexual nature."

To take them in order, the initial scene is indeed a murder. It is not, however, a rape. The scene is sexually suggestive, but there is no nudity and no specific sexual activity is shown on the screen except kissing. The scene, particularly the death of the young woman, is nonetheless shocking; I'm not sure that it's more shocking than what appears in many prime-time TV crime shows. I did watch the rest of it, and there are no more sexual scenes of any kind.

As for your second concern, it is technically true that "children" (meaning people under the age of eighteen) could check out the video, despite the fact that it is R-rated. As you may know, movie ratings are guidelines only. We do buy some such movies, in accordance with our policies, and over the past decade, I am aware of only one case in which a teenager deliberately checked out an R-rated movie from us. It too was a thriller (as opposed to something with more specifically sexual content). He also did it in direct opposition to his mother's clearly expressed direction.

In my experience, however, younger children are simply not interested in R-rated content, and it is very difficult for a child to check out, bring home, and watch a video without a parent knowing about it. On that basis, I have been reluctant to impose age-based restrictions on library materials. I read up on the ratings system one time, and found it to be very arbitrary. It seems to me that the "problem" of children's use of such materials just doesn't happen often enough to justify establishing new limits for all children.

As for your third concern, as I examine the video case, I see the following labels we have already put on it: the checkout period, with fine information; the cataloging and shelving labels; a warning reminding people not to leave the video out in the heat lest it be damaged and the patron have to pay for it; a label indicating that it belongs to the library; a reminder where to return the video; a date due sticker; a barcode; and finally, the cover itself, which is by that time so obscured that you can't even read the full description of the movie. On the other hand, all R-rated videos are so indicated on the video itself (on the lower left corner of the title information), not the case. As I review all this, I think we've utterly overdone the labels. We could probably get it down to the barcode, ownership sticker, and shelving label, then people could at least read the summary on the back.

In short, I've learned that people ignore labels, and are annoyed that they take up so much space as it is. One more warning, even if we got rid of all the others, isn't likely to do much good.

Finally, I thought I should tell you my judgment on the entire movie. It's quite good. I don't watch a lot of suspense/thriller movies, but this one was based on a popular book by David Baldacci, features a very fine and taut script by William Goldman, and some major actors who turned in some solid performances. Finally, the message is about the importance of family and the sometimes corrupting influence of power. It is certainly more suitable, in language and situation, for adults than for children, which is why we've cataloged it with our other adult videos. But again, I doubt that most children would find the situations of much interest.

As a parent myself, I do understand your disquiet over the ready accessibility of strong images in our culture. I've thought about this issue a lot, both as a father and as a librarian. I've concluded that direct conversation with your children is by far the most effective defense; and that governmental restrictions on content tend to raise many more problems than they solve.

After my review, I believe that the video is correctly placed in our collection. I do intend to review our labeling policy, however, but more with a view to reducing than expanding.

As spelled out in the policies sent to you earlier, you do have the option of appealing my decision to the board of trustees, my bosses. If you'd like to do that, let me know.

Meanwhile, thank you again for letting us know about your concerns.

Jagged Little Pill *(Music, Language)*

August 20, 2001

Dear Ms. Patron:

I did get around to listening to the entirety of Alanis Morissette's *Jagged Little Pill.* You are quite correct that there are two four-letter words that make rather sudden appearances. I see, too, that they are clearly listed in the lyrics. But I've never read the lyrics before listening to the music, and I doubt many other people do, either.

I've been in exactly the situation you describe: driving in the car with the kids, when suddenly language that you do not consider acceptable for your family comes blasting through the speakers. I do understand how awkward that can be.

Let me say, first, that I apologize. It is not the intent of the library either to shock you, or to initiate your children into the world of profanity.

I gave some time to your suggestion that we affix a label to the CD warning patrons of the presence of, as you put it, "words that may cause offense." I also did a fair amount of research into the practice of music labeling by the music industry.

To consider the last issue first, I found that music labeling has a long, and somewhat controversial history. It began in the early 1980s in the U.S., with the work of such people as Tipper Gore, Al Gore's wife. The intent was about what I think you intend: to give parents a clue about what their children might be listening to. After a series of intense, often confrontational Senate hearings in which both politicians and performers had their say, the Recording Industry Association of America (RIAA) adopted voluntary guidelines for the so-called Parental Advisory Label. This label states, "Parental Advisory: Explicit Content."

Some parents are concerned about language. Others have concerns about violence, misogyny, and the promotion of hate. Apparently all of this can be found in abundance in today's music. In 2000 the president of RIAA said that she didn't think the industry was following its own regulations very well. Since then, the pressure has been on—apparently to avoid federal legislation.

I found many statements about RIAA's concern about this issue, mainly from their web site at www.riaa.com. I did not find, nor can I obtain, a copy of just what the new, allegedly more strict guidelines, are supposed to be. At my local record store, I can find many CDs with the Explicit Content label. Morissette's is not among them.

So back to the idea of putting our own label on a CD. This presents the library with several dilemmas. First, how are we to know which words are used in a CD unless we listen to every one of them first? Second, what criteria should we use? Morissette used at least two words that we might agree are not best for children. Are two words enough? Who decides which other words? Third, we already catalog our holdings with various kinds of labels. We get complaints from patrons now who can't read the front or back of the cover art without dismantling the item. Where, exactly, would we put such a label?

I had several long discussions about this—both the concept and the physical demands of the CD—with my staff, and have concluded that I just don't have a good answer. Adult music—and that's where we've put Morissette's work—uses adult language. That seems to be fairly common. Like so much else in today's world—television and radio, for instance—music is one of those things that has to be monitored, and discussed, with young people in a way that I don't think was so common a generation ago.

So despite the fact that I don't find your request that we label such works as containing profanities at all unreasonable on the face of it, I think adopting the practice raises more problems than it solves. I have also attached some other library statements that speak to the more general concerns of censorship.

However, I think the issue of music labeling is worth some more public discussion. I'm going to write a newspaper column about it for next week. And I promise to keep thinking about it.

Finally, I have to say that this was the first time I've heard Alanis Morissette's music. Her voice—particularly on the unlisted track thirteen, at the very end—was absolutely enthralling. Life, it seems, is a mix.

Columns

Here are two examples of library newspaper columns. The first is the first column I wrote for the *Douglas County News Press*. Its purpose was to establish my voice as an author. It also offered me the opportunity to set a solid base for almost any story afterward: Intellectual freedom, ultimately, depends on the skill of literacy.

The second example refers to a time back in 2000, when "Dr. Laura" was in the first wave of those targeting the American Library Association and their stand against Internet filtering. This column ran first in the *Weekly News Chronicle*. I later submitted it to, and it ran in, the *Denver Post*.

"Literacy" (April 11, 1990)

Why read? After all, if it's news you want, either radio or TV will wrap it up in a couple of minutes. If you're looking for advice, there are probably a few people you trust—why not call them? If you're looking to just relax and have a good time, hey, jab in a video!

If this makes sense to you, if you're nodding your head, then chew on this: Every librarian has two nightmares, and you're the second, someone who can read but won't. What's our first nightmare? Someone who doesn't know how to read.

Before I came to Colorado I was a literacy tutor for over a year. My student was an alert, capable man, fifty-two years old. For twenty-five years he had worked at an automobile plant, running sophisticated electronic equipment. His memory was almost perfect. His ability to follow oral instructions was close to flawless. When I met John, I had trouble understanding just what I could do for him. Then I had him read me a "diagnostic" passage of text.

John read about as well as a beginning second grader. I was shocked. I asked him how many people knew about his reading problem. Just three, he said—an army sergeant, John's wife, and his daughter. He hadn't seen the sergeant in thirty years. His wife had died just recently. Once a week, he drove thirty miles to his daughter's house so she could go through his mail and pay his bills. That was partly the reason he had contacted the local literacy project—it was one thing to lean on his wife, he felt, something else to depend on his grown and married child.

Then, the automobile factory closed. John couldn't read a job application.

At first I couldn't believe that a reading problem that severe could go unnoticed for so long. But the functional illiterate quickly learn how not to be noticed. He doesn't have his glasses; could you read this to him? And that phenomenal memory—he never wrote anything down because he couldn't. He had to remember.

With John, I experienced one of the most intense pleasures a librarian can know. Once a week, I helped unlock the mind-boggling treasure that is a library. I gave him books, and they were welcomed as a starving man might welcome food. His joy in learning was keen and ravenous. He devoured suspense stories, newspapers, magazines, classics, even romances—with mounting ease and excitement.

I learned all over again what a precious, even magical thing a book is. And I learned how easy it is to teach motivated adults. They have a lifetime of experience to draw from and a need to know few children can match.

Mark Twain said, "There is no difference between a man who cannot read good books, and a man who will not."

Why read? Ask John.

"Dr. Laura and Internet Filtering" (January 12, 2000)

I don't exactly remember my parents telling me that it was wrong to steal. I knew I wasn't supposed to. Nevertheless, when I was maybe eight years old, I slipped into a Ben Franklin five-and-dime store, and swiped something. I forget what. But later on, my mother noticed that I was playing with a thing that did not fit into the narrow range of my allowance.

I survived, barely, the Inquisition—a savage unraveling of my flimsy lies. Then, pretty much by the ear, I was dragged back to the store.

There, with an air of combined shame and disgust, my mother made me confess my sin to the store management. I had to give back the merchandise. Management staff were suitably grave, but declined to press charges. This time.

I learned the lesson: Thou Shalt Not Steal. Not only because it made your mother mad at you and might result in jail, but—and this was the sermon on the trip home—because when I stole things, I was stealing the livelihood of the people who worked in the store. It was just No Way to Treat People. Decent people paid attention to the folks around them.

I got to thinking about this when a friend of mine gave me a write-up on one "Dr. Laura." She's a talk show host. Apparently Dr. Laura has been, for some time, very angry at the American Library Association in general, and public libraries in particular—especially those that don't use filtering software on their Internet terminals. The Douglas County Libraries, in case you were wondering, do not.

And in case you were wondering about this, a filtering company is one of the sponsors of Dr. Laura's radio show.

Once upon a time, or so I hear, Dr. Laura's message was personal responsibility. People would call up and tell her their dilemmas. Dr. Laura would insult and humiliate them. (Now that's entertainment!) But there was always a theme: Don't blame other people for your failures.

I have to admit that I don't listen to talk radio. But in general, I have to agree. People are responsible for their own lives.

But lately, Dr. Laura's mission is to force the evil empire of the American Library Association to require filtering software on each and every Internet terminal that children might access. The point is to protect kids from pornography. (And not, I feel sure, to boost the business of her sponsor.)

Quite aside from the technical issue of "Do filters work?" (or, for that matter, the awesome power of the ALA, or the constitutionality of computerized censorship), I have trouble squaring all this with Dr. Laura's earlier stance. My mom let me know that I wasn't supposed to steal. When I did, she didn't blame the store. She blamed me.

Similarly, parents can still tell their children not to look at, for instance, sexual content on public library terminals. If the child does anyhow, it seems to me that my mother was right. The library deserves, not blame, but an apology.

No store encourages people to steal. Some customers do anyhow. No library web site points to obscene material. Some people go looking for it.

Why should children—or, for that matter, adults—apologize for looking at sexy pictures at the library? Because they have misused a public resource. They have compromised public space. They have thoughtlessly complicated the jobs of library staff. This is, to be perfectly blunt, the behavior of louts.

Dr. Laura seems to think libraries should make it harder to misbehave. All I can say is, *my* mom wouldn't have bought that argument.

References and Resources

Reference List

American Library Association. 2002. "Book Burning in the 21st Century." http://www.ala.org/bbooks/bookburning21.html. Accessed January 11, 2007.

American Library Association. 2001. "Children and the Internet: Policies That Work." http://www.ala.org/ala/alsc/alscpubs/childrentheinternetpoliciesthatwork/ChildrenInternetArtOne.htm.

Berry, J. 2005. "LJ Talks to Rick Ashton, the Outgoing Director of the Denver Public Library." http://www.libraryjournal.com/article/CA6290565.html.

Center for Religion, Ethics, and Social Policy at Cornell University. "The Rise of the Religious Right in the Republican Party." http://www.theocracywatch.org/separation_church_state2.htm http://www.theocracywatch.org/texas_gop.htm.

DelFattore, J. 1992. *What Johnny Shouldn't Read: Textbook Censorship in America.* New Haven, CT: Yale University Press.

Geller, E. 1984. *Forbidden Books in American Public Libraries, 1876–1939: A Study in Cultural Change.* Wesport, CT: Greenwood Publishing Group.

Godwin, M. 1995. "Children, Child Abuse, and Cyberporn: A Primer for Clear Thinkers." http://www.eff.org//Censorship/kids_and_cyberporn_godwin.article.

Hentoff, N. 1980. *The First Freedom.* New York: Delacorte.

Kramnick, I., and R. Moore. 1996. *The Godless Constitution: The Case Against Religious Correctness.* New York: W. W. Norton & Company.

Levy, L. 1985. *Emergence of a Free Press.* New York: Oxford University Press.

Lipscomb, A., and A. Bergh, ed. 1903–1904. *The Writings of Thomas Jefferson, Memorial Edition.* Washington, DC: Thomas Jefferson Memorial Association.

McMurtrie, Douglas C. 1943. *The Book: The Story of Printing & Bookmaking.* New York: Oxford University Press.

Office for Intellectual Freedom. 2002. *Intellectual Freedom Manual,* 6th edition. Chicago: American Library Association.

Peterson, M., ed. 1994. *Thomas Jefferson: Writings.* New York: Library of America.

Robbins, L. 1997. *Censorship and the American Library: The American Library Association's Response to Threats to Intellectual Freedom, 1939–1969.* Westport, CT: Greenwood Publishing Group.

Samek, T. 2001. *Intellectual Freedom and Social Responsibility in American Librarianship, 1967–1974.* Jefferson, NC: McFarland.

Schweber, H. 2003. *Speech, Conduct and The First Amendment.* New York: P. Lang.

Strauss, W., and Howe, N. 1990. *Generations: The History of America's Future, 1584–2069.* New York: Morrow.

Strauss, W., and Howe, N. 1997. *The Fourth Turning: An American Prophecy.* New York: Broadway Books.

Tedford, T. 1997. *Freedom of Speech in the United States.* State College, PA: Strata Publishing.

Van Biema, D. "Kingdom Come." (August 4, 1997). *Time Australia, 31,* p. 48–56.

Walker, J. 1997. "The Government of the United States of America Is Not, in Any Sense Founded on the Christian Religion." http://nobeliefs.com/Tripoli.htm.

Werhan, K. 2004. *Freedom of Speech: A Reference Guide to the United States Constitution.* Westport, CT: Greenwood Publishing Group.

Williams, R., and M. Kamien. 2002. "Okham's Razor: Book Burning and the Reflex." http://www.abc.net.au/rn/science/ockham/stories/s32651.htm. Accessed January 11, 2007.

Intellectual Freedom Resources

If, or when, your library receives a challenge, you may seek some legal assistance or advice. Below is a list of some reliable and reputable sources of support. I am indebted to the Colorado Association of Libraries Intellectual Freedom Committee for the links and format.

American Library Association Office for Intellectual Freedom
50 East Huron Street
Chicago, Illinois 60611
800-545-2433, ext. 4223
http://www.ala.org/oif

The Office for Intellectual Freedom is charged with implementing American Library Association (ALA) policies concerning the concept of intellectual freedom as embodied in the Library Bill of Rights, the association's basic policy on free access to libraries and library materials. The goal of the office is to educate librarians and the general public about the nature and importance of intellectual freedom in libraries.

Freedom to Read Foundation
50 East Huron Street
Chicago, Illinois 60611
800-545-2433 ext. 4224
http://www.ala.org/ala/ourassociation/othergroups/ftrf/freedomread
foundation.htm

The First Amendment to the U.S. Constitution guarantees all individuals the right to express their ideas without governmental interference, and to read and listen to the ideas of others. The Freedom to Read Foundation was established to promote and defend this right; to foster libraries and institutions wherein every individual's First Amendment freedoms are fulfilled; and to support the right of libraries to include in their collections and make available any work that they may legally acquire.

The American Civil Liberties Union
125 Broad Street, 18th Floor
New York, NY 10004
http://www.aclu.org/
http://www.aclu.org/affiliates/
    The American Civil Liberties Union is the nation's foremost advocate of individual rights—litigating, legislating, and educating the public on a broad array of issues affecting individual freedom in the United States.

People For the American Way
2000 M Street, NW, Suite 400
Washington, DC 20036
800-326-7329
http://www.pfaw.org
    People For the American Way and People For the American Way Foundation work to protect the heart of democracy and the soul of the nation. In Congress and state capitals, in classrooms and in libraries, in courthouses and houses of worship, on the airwaves and on the printed page, on sidewalks and in cyberspace, we work to promote full citizen participation in our democracy and safeguard the principles of our Constitution from those who threaten the American dream.

Index

Photo compliments of Beth Seliga/www.3catsphoto.com

About the Author

James LaRue has been the director of the Douglas County Libraries (Castle Rock, Colorado) since 1990. In addition to the weekly newspaper column he's written for more than twenty years, he has contributed editorials to the *Denver Post*, appeared on National Public Radio, written for most major library periodicals, and is a popular keynote speaker for various state library associations. His awards include Colorado Librarian of the Year (1998), the Julie J. Boucher Award for Intellectual Freedom (2000), Castle Rock Business Person of the Year (2003), and the National Council of Teachers of English/Support for the Learning and Teaching of English Intellectual Freedom Award (2004).